THE BALKANS

MARK MAZOWER

THE BALKANS

A Short History

A MODERN LIBRARY CHRONICLES BOOK

THE MODERN LIBRARY

NEW YORK

Acknowledgments

I am deeply grateful to Phil Nord for allowing me to spend two years at Princeton, where I have been blessed with an extraordinary group of friends and colleagues. My thanks in particular for their comments, advice, guidance and criticism in connection with this project to: Peter Brown, Marwa Elshakry, Laura Engelstein, Bill Jordan, Tia Kolbaba, Liz Lunbeck, Arno Mayer, Ken Mills and Gyan Prakash. Molly Greene and Heath Lowry patiently introduced me to Ottoman realities; Polymeris Voglis and Dimitris Livanios made many valuable suggestions and criticisms. In London, Peter Mandler gave me advice and assistance. Johanna Weber offered huge encouragement, and challenged my prose line by line: my debt to her is beyond words. My thanks too to Nicholas Dirks and Tony Molho for opportunities to try out portions of my argument at Columbia and Brown Universities, and to Fergus Bremner for his refreshing and nourishing ideas. I am indebted to the British Academy and the Leverholme Trust for their generous support of my work. Over many years, Dimitri Gondicas has turned the Program in Hellenic Studies at Princeton into a major center for research and intellectual exchange. To him, as token of my long-standing gratitude, admiration and deep affection, I dedicate this book.

CONTENTS

1683	Unsuccessful Ottoman assault on Vienna
1699	Treaty of Carlowitz
1711–1715	Phanariot princes begin rule in Danubian Principalities
1718	Treaty of Passarowitz
1736–1739	Russo/Austrian-Turkish War
1768–1774	Russo-Turkish War
1770	Revolt in the Peloponnese
1774	Treaty of Kutschuk-Kainardji
1787–1792	Russo/Austrian-Turkish War
1797	End of the Venetian Republic
1804	First Serbian Uprising
1815	Second Serbian Uprising
1821	Greek War of Independence begins
1827	Battle of Navarino
1830	Greek independence
1839	Reform legislation in Ottoman empire
1858	Unification of Danubian Principalities [Romania]
1870	Creation of the Exarchate of the Bulgarian Orthodox Church
1877–1878	Russo-Turkish War
1878	Treaty of San Stefano, superseded by Treaty of Berlin; results in autonomy for Bulgaria; Serbia, Montenegro and Romania recognized as independent states; Cyprus occupied by British; and Austria-Hungary occupies Bosnia-Hercegovina
1893	Foundation of Internal Macedonian Revolutionary Organization
1903	Ilinden Uprising
1908	Young Turk revolt; Bosnian annexation crisis

1912	First Balkan War; Albania recognized as independent state (its boundaries fixed 1921)
1913	Second Balkan War
1914–1918	First World War
1918	Kingdom of Serbs, Croats and Slovenes [Yugoslavia] established
1919–1922	Greco-Turkish War in Anatolia
1923	Treaty of Lausanne between Greece and Turkey and exchange of populations; Italian bombardment of Corfu
1939	Italian invasion of Albania
1940	Romania forced to cede territory to USSR, Hungary and Bulgaria; Italian invasion of Greece
1941	German invasion of Yugoslavia and Greece
1941–1944	Axis occupation; creation of Independent State of Croatia
1944–1945	German withdrawal from the Balkans
1946–1949	Greek civil war
1948	Tito-Stalin split
1967–1974	Dictatorship in Greece
1980	Tito dies
1989	Downfall of Communist regimes throughout Eastern Europe
1990–1991	Fighting in Slovenia and Croatia
1992–1995	War in Bosnia
1999	War in Kosovo between NATO states and Serbia

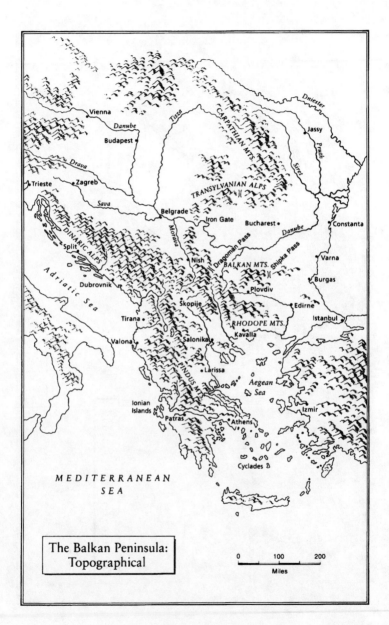

The Balkan Peninsula: Topographical

0   100   200
         Miles

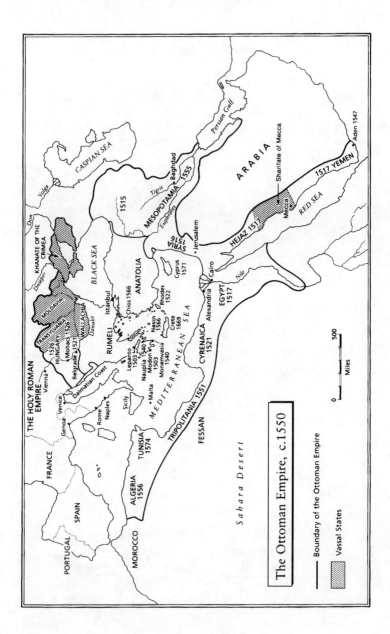

The Ottoman Empire, c.1550

Boundary of the Ottoman Empire

Vassal States

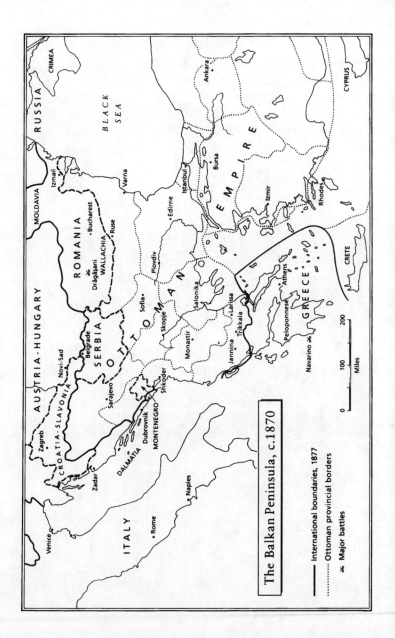

The Balkan Peninsula, c.1870

International boundaries, 1877
Ottoman provincial borders
Major battles

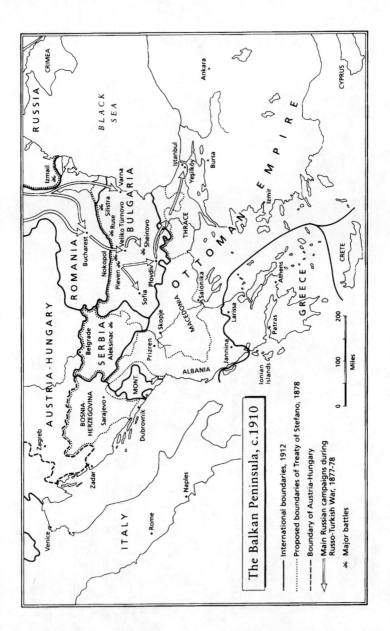

The Balkan Peninsula, c.1910

——— International boundaries, 1912

·········· Proposed boundaries of Treaty of Stefano, 1878

– – – Boundary of Austria-Hungary

⟹ Main Russian campaigns during Russo-Turkish War, 1877–78

⚔ Major battles

| 0 | 100 | 200 |
| Miles |

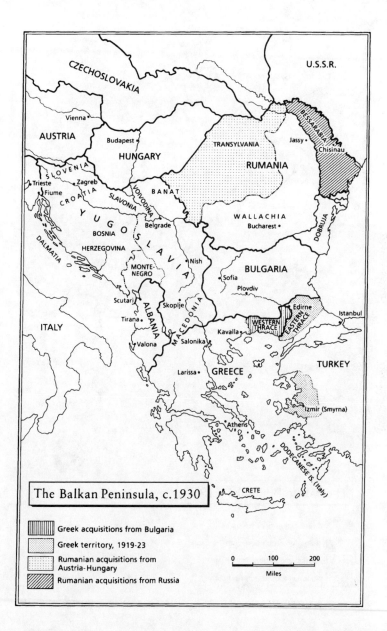

The Balkan Peninsula, c.1930

|||||| Greek acquisitions from Bulgaria

Greek territory, 1919-23

Rumanian acquisitions from Austria-Hungary

Rumanian acquisitions from Russia

0   100   200
         Miles

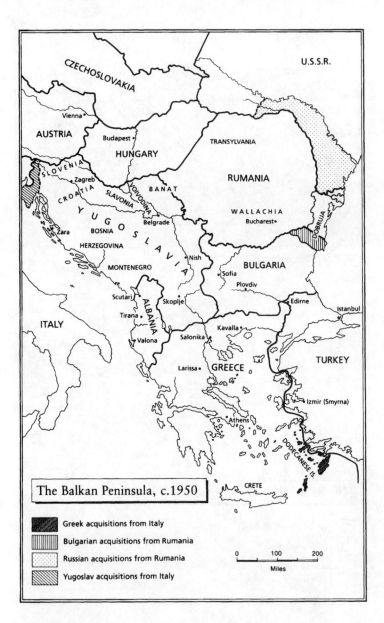

The Balkan Peninsula, c.1950

Greek acquisitions from Italy
Bulgarian acquisitions from Rumania
Russian acquisitions from Rumania
Yugoslav acquisitions from Italy

0   100   200

Miles

The Balkan Peninsula, c.2000

—— International boundaries

0   100   200
        Miles

INTRODUCTION: NAMES

> The reputation, name and appearance, the usual measure and weight
> of a thing, what it counts for—originally almost always wrong and
> arbitrary ... all this grows from generation unto generation, merely
> because people believe in it, until it gradually grows to be part of the
> thing and turns into its very body. What at first was appearance
> becomes in the end, almost invariably, the essence and effective as
> such.   —FRIEDRICH NIETZSCHE[1]

At the end of the twentieth century, people spoke as if the
Balkans had existed forever. However, two hundred years earlier, they had not yet come into being. It was not the Balkans but
"Rumeli" that the Ottomans ruled, the formerly "Roman" lands
that they had conquered from Constantinople. The Sultan's
educated Christian Orthodox subjects referred to themselves
as "Romans" ("Romaioi"), or more simply as "Christians." To
Westerners, familiar with classical regional terms such as Macedonia, Epirus, Dacia and Moesia, the term "Balkan" conveyed
little. "My expectations were raised," wrote one traveler in 1854,
"by hearing that we were about to cross a *Balkan;* but I discovered
ere long that this high-sounding title denotes only a ridge which
divides the waters, or a mountain pass, without its being a necessary consequence that it offer grand or romantic scenery."[2]

"Balkan" was initially a name applied to the mountain
range better known to the classically trained Western traveler
as ancient Haemus, passed en route from central Europe to
Constantinople. In the early nineteenth century, army officers

like the Earl of Albemarle explored its little-known slopes. "The interior of the Balcan," wrote a Prussian diplomat who crossed it in 1833, "has been little explored, and but a few, accurate measurements of elevation have been undertaken." Little had changed twenty years later, when Giacomo August Jochmus's "Notes on a Journey into the Balkan, or Mount Haemus" was read to the Royal Geographical Society. It was across these mountains that the Russian army advanced on Constantinople in 1829 and again in 1877. "The crossing of the Balkans," wrote the author of a popular history of the Russo-Turkish War of the latter year, "must be reckoned one of the most remarkable achievements of the war."[3]

By this time, a handful of geographers had already stretched the word to refer to the entire region, mostly on the erroneous assumption that the Balkan range ran right across the peninsula of southeastern Europe, much as the Pyrenees demarcated the top of the Iberian. In the eighteenth century, geographical knowledge of the Turkish domains was very vague; as late as 1802, John Pinkerton noted that "recent maps of these regions are still very imperfect." Most scholars, including the Greek authors of the earliest study from the area, used the much commoner term "European Turkey," and references to "the Balkans" remained scarce long into the nineteenth century. They are, for instance, absent in the writings of the savant Ami Boué, whose minute exploration of the entire region—*La Turquie d'Europe* of 1840—set standards of accuracy and detail not matched for generations.[4]

Nor before the 1880s were there many references to "Balkan" peoples either. The world of Orthodoxy encompassed Greek and Slav alike, and it took time for ethnographic and political distinctions between the various Orthodox populations to emerge. In 1797, the revolutionary firebrand Rhigas Velestinlis, inspired by the French Revolution, predicted the downfall of the Sultan and proclaimed the need for a "Hellenic

Republic" in which all the peoples of "Rumeli, Asia Minor, the Archipelago, Moldavia and Wallachia" would be recognized as citizens, despite their "different races and religions." In Rhigas's vast future republic, Greek was to be the language not only of learning but also of government. As late as the 1850s informed commentators were still scoffing at "superficial observers, who consider the Slavonic races as 'Greek' because the great majority of them are of the 'Greek' religion." Even the German scholar Karl Ritter proposed calling the whole region south of the Danube the "Halbinsel Griechenland" (Greek peninsula). "Till quite lately," wrote the British historian E. A. Freeman in 1877, "all the Orthodox subjects of the Turk were in most European eyes looked on alike as Greeks."[5]

Well after the unmistakable rise of Slav nationalisms, it was hard to discern what pattern of states and peoples would succeed the Turks. Some commentators imagined a variety of self-governing Christian polities under overall Ottoman suzerainty, while others foresaw the partition of the region between a Greek state and a South Slav federation. Almost none anticipated the process of fragmentation that actually occurred. "Even in our days," remarked a French writer in 1864, "how often have I heard people ask who the Christian populations of Turkey belong to—Russia, Austria, France? And when some dreamers replied: These populations belong to themselves—what amusement, what pity at such utopianism."[6]

Through the eighteenth and nineteenth centuries, "Turkey in Europe" was the favored geographical coin of the day. But by the 1880s, the days of "Turkey in Europe" were evidently numbered. Successor states—Greece, Bulgaria, Serbia, Romania and Montenegro—had emerged during the nineteenth century as contenders to carve up what remained. Between 1878 and 1908, diplomatic conferences whittled away Ottoman territory, and subjected what remained to Great Power oversight. Western travelers, journalists and propagandists flocked to the region and popularized the new, broader use of the term "Balkans." By the time of the outbreak of the First Balkan War in 1912—which ended Ottoman rule in Europe (outside the immediate hinterland of Constantinople)—it had become common currency. Purists were annoyed. One German geographer talked crossly of "the southeast European—or as people increasingly say, perpetuating the error of half a century—the *Balkan* peninsula." A Bulgarian expert complained about "this region... [being] wrongly called the Balkan peninsula." But the tide was against such pedantry. In less than half a century, largely as a result of sudden military and diplomatic changes, a new geographical concept rooted itself in everyday parlance. By 1917, a standard history of the Eastern Question talked about the "lands which the geographers of the last generation described as 'Turkey in Europe' but for which political changes have compelled us to seek a new name. The name generally given to that segment is 'the Balkan Peninsula' or simply, 'the Balkans.' "[7]

From the very start the Balkans was more than a geographical concept. The term, unlike its predecessors, was loaded with negative connotations—of violence, savagery, primitivism—to an extent for which it is hard to find a parallel. "Why 'savage Europe'?" asked the journalist Harry de Windt in his 1907 book of the same name. "Because... the term accurately describes the wild and lawless countries between the Adriatic and Black Seas." Attuned to a history of revolt and revenge stretching back almost a century and climaxing after 1900 in the terrorist bombings of the Internal Macedonian Revolutionary Organization, the Serbian regicide of 1903 and the widespread massacres carried out by all sides during the Balkan Wars, Europe quickly came to associate the region with violence and bloodshed. A decade of further fighting—ending in 1922 with the Greek defeat by the Turks in Asia Minor, and the forced population exchange of nearly two million refugees—did little to alter the picture.

True, the Balkan peoples now ruled themselves, as so many Western advocates on their behalf had wished. But what was the result? A panoply of small, unviable, mutually antagonistic and internally intolerant states. This looked exactly like the *kleinstaaterei* that opponents of the unrestricted spread of national states had feared. Liberals found it hard to reconcile their happy ideal of national self-determination with the realities of a fragmented and destabilized world. In the case of new states such as Germany and Italy, nineteenth-century nationalism had welded together tiny antiquated statelets into larger and economically more rational units; in the Balkans the outcome had been the opposite.[8]

Between the wars, novelists and film directors turned the region into a stage set for exotic thrillers of corruption, quick killing and easy crime. For Eric Ambler, in *The Mask of Dimitrios,* the Balkans symbolized the moral decay of interwar Europe itself. For the less sophisticated Agatha Christie, in her 1925 *The Secret of Chimneys,* it provided a home for the villainous Boris Anchoukoff, who came from "one of the Balkan states.... Principal rivers, unknown. Principal mountains, also unknown, but fairly numerous. Capital, Ekarest. Population, chiefly brigands. Hobby, assassinating kings and having revolutions." As Rebecca West wrote at the start of her travelogue *Black Lamb and Grey Falcon:* "Violence was, indeed, all I knew of the Balkans: all I knew of the South Slavs." Jacques Tourneur's 1942 film noir, *Cat People,* went even further and turned the Balkans—through the troubled persona of the film's Serbian heroine—into the seedbed of an "ancient sin" that turned humans into lethal sexual predators who threatened to destroy the "normal, happy lives" of ordinary Americans.[9]

In the postwar era, some of these clichés became less powerful. The Balkans disappeared from Western consciousness during the Cold War, and the Iron Curtain ran through southeastern Europe, separating Greece from its Communist neighbors. Albania became virtually impenetrable. Tito's Yugoslavia was idolized by American policymakers and by the New Left in Europe; the language of international non-alignment and of workers' self-management at home fell on receptive ears abroad. Nicolae Ceausescu's rule in Romania was known more for its pronounced anti-Sovietism in foreign policy than for its extreme repression of its own population. In general, Greece became a marginal part of "the West," while the other Balkan states formed the least studied part of Communist Eastern Europe. Mass tourism brought millions to the region's beaches and ski slopes, and turned peasant culture into after-dinner entertainment. The picturesque replaced the violent, and the worst problems most tourists anticipated were poor roads and unfamiliar toilets.

These were the benefits of the long peace that fell over Europe with the Cold War. To many today they appear not only distant but illusory, a hiatus in which the true character of the Balkans was temporarily obscured. Since the collapse of communism, it has become easier to see southeastern Europe again as a single entity, but its well-established derogatory connotations have also reemerged. Indeed, the fighting precipitated by the breakup of Yugoslavia has probably left these more entrenched in the popular imagination than ever: it is now not only Tito and communism that are blamed for mass violence, but ethnic diversity itself and long-standing historical cleavages between religions and cultures. It is hard to find people with anything good to say about the region, harder still to discuss it beyond good or evil. Whether it is possible to take a fresh look at the Balkans, without seeing them refracted through the prism of "the Balkans" we have lived with for so long, is the main challenge of this work.

———

If the intellectual history of Western stereotypes of the Balkans were no more than one century old, it would be hard to explain the grip they still have on us. But the term, though of relatively recent vintage, rests upon a foundation of other associations that reach more deeply into Western thought. One of these is the tension between Orthodox and Catholic Christianity that was crystallized by the Crusaders' sacking of Byzantine Constantinople in 1204. But more important still is surely the deep rift of incomprehension that lies between the worlds of Christianity and Islam, which for more than a millennium—from the seventh century until at least the end of the seventeenth—were locked in a complex struggle for territory and minds in Europe.

To the first *jihad,* which swept Muslim culture into an area extending from Spain (and much of Africa) to the borders of India and China, Christendom responded with the Iberian *reconquista,* the recovery of lands in southern Italy and, most important, the Crusades. The "Holy Wars of the Mediterranean" may have been ultimately, in the words of Eric Christiansen "a sad waste of time, money and life." But though two centuries of struggle against the Saracens failed to regain Jerusalem for Christianity, they contributed enormously to strengthening a tradition of martial intolerance in Christian Europe to heretics, pagans and above all to Muslims. While Muslim polities accepted non-Muslims as subjects—non-Muslims were always a majority of the population in the Ottoman Balkans—Christian states expelled Muslims (and strictly controlled the settlement of small communities of Jews from medieval times on) and regarded them as a threat.[10]

The second Islamic campaign against Christendom was spearheaded by a central Asian nomadic people, the Turks. Between the eleventh and the seventeenth centuries, Turkic peoples gradually overran and defeated the Byzantine empire, conquering Christian outposts in the eastern Aegean, and round the rim of the Black Sea, eventually pushing up through Hungary to the Germanic heartlands of central

Europe. Twice, Ottoman armies besieged Vienna. Christians interpreted the fall of Constantinople in 1453 as proof of the degeneracy of Orthodoxy, the ultimate failure of Byzantium as an imperial system, and a divine punishment for men's sins. As Turkish ships cruised off the coast of Italy, pious Catholics were told to "pray for the undoing of Islam." The Ottoman dynasty might have seen itself as the successor to the universal monarchies of Rome and Byzantium, "the shadow of God on earth." But to many Christians, like the Elizabethan historian Richard Knolles, it was the latest incarnation of the Islamic peril and "the present terror of the world."[11]

For all the religious antipathy between Christian and Muslim, sixteenth-century Europeans respected and feared the power, reach and efficiency of the Turks. The "Gran Signore," as the Ottoman Sultan was commonly known, was regarded as perhaps the most powerful ruler in the known world. Renaissance observers described him as the successor to Alexander the Great and the Roman emperors, and drew unfavorable contrasts with the disorganized state of Christian armies. In 1525, Christendom's always shaky united front broke down when Francis I, the king of France and "Eldest Son of the Church" sought an alliance with Suleiman the Great against the Holy Roman Emperor. "The sacrilegious union of the Lily and the Crescent" was the beginning of a long association between Catholic France and the Turks. The Venetians too were impressed by the seemingly boundless territorial and human resources of an imperial machine built for war. Their ambassador Marco Minio had already warned in 1521 that the "Gran Signore seems to have in his grasp the keys to all Christendom."[12]

For Thomas Fuller in 1639, the Sultan's empire was "the greatest and best-compacted that the sunne ever saw. Take sea and land together ... and from Buda in the West to Tauris in the East, it stretcheth about three thousand miles.... It lieth in the heart of the world, like a bold champion bidding defiance to all his borderers, commanding the most fruitfull countreys of Europe, Asia and Africa." With two metropolises—Constantinople and Cairo—which awed visitors by their size and dwarfed London, Paris, Amsterdam and Rome, its magnificence overshadowed its squabbling neighbors in Christendom. And its power attracted as well as repelled Europeans. "Seeing how many goe from us to them," commented Sir Henry Blount on Christian converts to Islam, "and how few of theirs to us; it appeares of what consequence the prosperity of a cause is to draw men unto it."[13]

Gradually this tone of respect for the Ottoman regime began to disappear. From the second half of the seventeenth century onward, even before Montesquieu's writings on the theme appeared, Ottoman rule was increasingly described as a "tyranny" or a "despotism"; earlier allusions to its religious tolerance diminished; and there was a growing emphasis on its lack of legitimacy, its reliance on corruption, extortion and injustice, and the inevitability of its eventual decline.

This shift in sentiment took place at a time when the balance of power between the Turks and their opponents was visibly altering and it looked as though Ottoman armies were approaching their limits. Christian Europe itself was growing stronger thanks to the growth of trade and empires across the Atlantic, the emergence of mercantile capitalism and the construction of a new state system after the Thirty Years War. In particular, the rise of Russia and Habsburg Austria as military threats capable of going on the offensive against the Ottomans fundamentally altered the balance of power in eastern Europe and the Black Sea region. From the second siege of Vienna in 1683, Ottoman power in Europe waned: Habsburg armies captured Hungary, Croatia and adjacent areas, which they repopulated with Christian settlers and turned into a military frontier zone. The empire was also becoming weaker internally. Ottoman officials themselves noted the central state's growing loss of control over the provinces; mourning for the golden age of the sixteenth century turned into a topos in Ottoman political literature. Life in much of the empire, and certainly in the Balkans, became less secure.[14]

Broad shifts in values accompanied these political and economic developments. After the religious wars of the seventeenth century, the rise of science and the Enlightenment brought a new secularism to Europe that unified elite culture and made the politico-religious structure of the Ottoman empire seem old-fashioned. From this point on there emerges a Western condemnation of overweening religious power—applied to corrupt Orthodox prelates as much as to Islamic "fanatics"—which has lasted into the present. In the writings of travelers, pundits and philosophers, powerful new polarities emerge—between civilized West and barbarous East, between freedom-loving Europe and despotic Orient. Sensual, slow-moving, dreamlike, the latter acted as a mirror to the self-regarding Western visitor.[15]

The Balkans themselves occupied an intermediate cultural zone between Europe and Asia—in Europe but not of it. Nineteenth-century travelers had a far sharper and more value-laden sense than their predecessors that they were leaving Europe for Asia the minute they crossed into Ottoman lands. Standing in 1875 on the banks of the river Sava, the border between Habsburg Croatia and Ottoman Bosnia, the youthful Arthur Evans began "to realize in what a new world we were. The Bosniacs themselves speak of the other side of the Save [*sic*] as 'Europe' and they are right; for to all intents and purposes a five minutes' voyage transports you into Asia. Travelers who have seen the Turkish provinces of Syria, Armenia, or Egypt, when they enter Bosnia, are at once surprised at finding the familiar sights of Asia and Africa reproduced in a province of European Turkey." Westerners noted the insecurity of private property, the mysteries of Ottoman law and the sharp and all-important distinction between ruling and subject religions. Above all, they were struck by a set of aesthetic, almost theatrical impressions—the unexpected colors, smells, mixtures of peoples. Landing in Préveza, opposite the Ionian islands, in 1812, the young Henry Holland wrote: "Entering these regions, the scene is suddenly shifted, and you have before your eyes a new species of beings, with all those gaudy appendages of oriental character and scenery which have so long delighted the imagination in the tales of the East. The uniform habits of the Turk, derived from his religion and other circumstances, render this change almost as remarkable in the first Turkish town you may enter, as in those much further removed from the vicinity of the European nations." One century later, a young Russian journalist—later to achieve fame as Leon Trotsky—looked out of his carriage window as he traveled by rail from Budapest to Belgrade on the eve of the First Balkan War, and enthused: "The East! The East!—what a mixture of faces, costumes, ethnic types and cultural levels!"[16]

The disconcerting interpenetration of Europe and Asia, West and East, finds its way into most descriptions of the Balkans in modern times. Europe is seen as a civilizing force, a missile embedding itself in the passive matter of the Orient. Travelers routinely comment on signs of "European" life, such as houses with glass windows, cutlery, cabarets or hotels with billiard rooms. Balkan cities are usually described as having a European façade behind which hides an oriental—meaning picturesque but dirty, smelly, wooden and unplanned—reality. Railways are European, cart tracks are not; technology is definitely European, but not religious observance. The social fabric is almost always divided into a modernizing surface and a traditional substance. Oriental realities—the power of religion, the prevalence of agrarian poverty—are assumed to be phenomena that have not changed for centuries. By the end of the nineteenth century, as numerous accounts testify, it was virtually impossible for Western travelers—exposed to the heady delights and sensuous Orientalism of writers such as Pierre Loti—*not* to see the Balkans in this way.

Diplomatically—and despite the link with France—the Ottoman empire was long regarded as lying outside the European concert of powers. It had not been represented at the Congress of Vienna, for instance, in 1815 and was excluded by commentators on international law from "the Christian family of nations." Only *realpolitik*—produced by the empire's own evident decline, and the worrying rise of Russia—brought it in. Having essentially fought the Crimean War to save the Turks from the Russians, the victorious powers in 1856 finally declared "the Sublime Porte admitted to participate in the advantages of the Public Law and System of Europe." But in return the Porte was compelled to introduce reforms with regard to property, justice and religious equality that the Christian powers insisted were necessary for a modern, civilized state.[17]

The Turks themselves were never accepted as Europeans. In the increasingly racialized vocabulary of the nineteenth century, they were "Asiatics," "nomads" and "barbarians" ruling over the "lands where European civilization had its birth." "The Turks," wrote Lord John Russell in 1828, "appear to be distinguished from the nations which occupy the rest of Europe in nearly every circumstance." Even for R. G. Latham, among the most levelheaded of Victorian ethnographers, "the Turk is European, as the New Englander is American, i.e. not strictly." While Latham poured scorn on the idea that the Turks were "newcomers" to Europe, or "Asiatic" in any meaningful sense, he felt their religion made them "impracticable members of the European system." Muslims were widely regarded as more prone to acts of barbarism than their Christian subjects. "No war, ancient or modern," wrote an American diplomat in 1842, "was ever carried on with such unrelenting fury and such cruelty as the war against the Greeks by the Turks. It is a matter of astonishment that the Christian nations of Europe could have so long remained silent spectators of its atrocities." Despite the writings of men like George Finlay, whose history of the Greek War of Independence pulled no punches in describing a mutual "war of extermination," in the popular imagination the violence ran only one way. This one-sided outrage was harnessed effectively by Gladstone in his denunciations of the "Bulgarian horrors": it proved, on the whole, impervious to any evidence that Christians too committed atrocities, or on occasions deliberately provoked them. "When a Moslem kills a Moslem, it does not count," was how Edith Durham summed up Western attitudes. "When a Christian kills a Moslem, it is a righteous act; when a Christian kills a Christian it is an error of judgment better not talked about; it is only when a Moslem kills a Christian that we arrive at a full-blown atrocity."[18]

Christian Europe's blindness to Muslim victims overlooked the huge movements of populations triggered off by Ottoman decline. "People often talk in the West about transporting all the Turks, in other words Muslims, to Asia in order to turn Turkey in Europe into a uniquely Christian empire," Ami Boué had written in 1854. "This would be a decree as inhumane as the expulsion of the Jews from Spain, or of Protestants from France, and indeed scarcely feasible since the Europeans always forget that in Turkey in Europe the Muslims are mostly Slavs or Albanians, whose right to the land is as ancient as that of their Christian compatriots." Yet, according to one estimate, nearly 5 million Muslims were driven from former Ottoman lands in the Balkans and the Black Sea region in the century after 1821; from the Balkans themselves between 1.7 and 2 million Muslims immigrated voluntarily or involuntarily between 1878 and 1913 to what would later become the republic of Turkey. The Turkish language declined as a regional lingua franca, urban settlements were taken over by Christian incomers and Ottoman buildings were deliberately demolished or left to rot. The dynamiting of mosques and other architectural masterpieces in Bosnia-Hercegovina in the early 1990s was thus the continuation in an extreme form of a process of de-Islamicization that had begun decades earlier.[19]

When the Ottoman empire in the Balkans collapsed in 1912–1913, many in the West saw this as the final expulsion of "Asian" power from Europe and the triumph of the religious and racial vigor of Christendom. According to the American journalist Frederick Moore in the *National Geographic,* the Asiatic Turks had blighted their European subjects by imposing Islamic rule upon them. They had tried to invigorate their own racial stock through conversion, but had ultimately been unable to prevail over the biologically superior European breeds they ruled. Now "[the Turk] will make his way back to Asia as he came, centuries ago, little changed by his association with the peoples of Europe—whom he has kept as he found them, in a medieval condition, with all the barbarity of medieval Europe, with all its picturesqueness, its color, squalor and unthinking faith." As for the future, Moore predicted little change among the empire's former rulers since "[the Turk] is a Moslem, and the soul of the true Moslem is indifferent to progress." But "for the enlarged Balkan States it seems safe to predict rapid development along modern lines, for we have seen how all of them under great difficulties have already fulfilled partially, at least, their aspirations to adopt the civilizing institutions of Europe."[20]

Moore's prediction was entirely in line with commonplace liberal expectations of the relative civilizational capacities of Islamic and Christian peoples. It reflected the reasoning that had created powerful and influential lobbies in the rest of Europe for Bulgarian, Serbian and Greek liberation from Ottoman rule. But it was precisely this attitude that bred the almost inevitable disappointment which followed. As early as 1836, after Balkan nationalism's first triumph, a French traveler to Greece had registered the emotional shift. "The Greeks as slaves of the Turks were to be pitied," he wrote. "The Greeks once free merely horrify. Their life is a sequence of thefts and assaults, fires and assassinations their pastime." In similar fashion, the liberal optimism of 1912 was quickly and even more rudely to be dashed. The victorious Balkan states, fresh from beating the Ottoman army, immediately turned on one another in the Second Balkan War. News emerged of the brutality waged by their regular armies against civilians, especially in Macedonia, Kosovo and the borders of Montenegro. "That's how all this looks when you see it close up," reported Trotsky. "Meat is rotting, human flesh as well as the flesh of oxen; villages have become pillars of fire; men are exterminating 'persons not under twelve years of age'; everyone is being brutalized, losing their human aspect."[21]

Above all, in June 1914, came the assassination of the Archduke Franz Ferdinand by the Serbian nationalist student Gavrilo Princip. The second Bosnian crisis, and the third Balkan war, of the twentieth century turned into the continental bloodbath that finally destroyed Europe's old order. For this, if nothing else, the Balkans were henceforth cursed in the European consciousness. Only those most committed to one or other of these small nations continued to argue that they were worth supporting. Even fewer bothered to argue that they should not be loaded down with the cultural assumptions of the West but understood on their own terms.

———

A truer and less jaundiced understanding of the Balkans requires us to try to unravel the ways in which attitudes to the region have been shaped not only by events that took place there but by more sweeping narratives of the development of European identity and civilization. The basic historiographical challenge is how to fit the centuries of Ottoman rule into the story of the continent as a whole. For many eminent scholars of Europe the answer has been obvious. Sir John Marriott begins his sober history of the Eastern Question with the stark assertion that "the primary and most essential factor in the problem is the presence, embedded in the living flesh of Europe, of an alien substance. That substance is the Ottoman Turk." Ottoman rule, in other words, sundered the Balkans from the rest of the continent and ushered in a new dark ages for the region, since—in the words of Polish historian Oskar Halecki—"throughout the whole course of European history in its proper sense, Europe was practically identical with Christendom." The fact that before the Turks, the region formed part of the only marginally less despised Byzantine empire simply reinforced this way of looking at the problem.[22]

Not everyone buys this straightforward equation of Europe with (Catholic) Christianity. Arnold Toynbee and Nicolae Iorga, the eminent Romanian historian, have both argued—following, after all, the claims of Mehmed the Conqueror himself—that it was actually the Ottoman empire which was the successor to the "universal state" of Byzantine Orthodoxy. Iorga in particular suggested that there had been a "Byzantium after Byzantium" surviving under the rule of the sultans. But this assertion of the affinities that might bind Christianity and Islam has largely fallen on deaf ears. Many more scholars—and probably the mass of popular opinion—have followed Halecki, who insists that "from the European point of view, it must be observed that the Ottoman empire, completely alien to its European subjects in origin, tradition and religion, far from integrating them in a new type of culture, brought them nothing but a degrading foreign dominance which interrupted for approximately four hundred years their participation in European history."

Following this logic, successor states in the Balkans look back to the medieval or classical past for their national roots, and encourage their historians to pass over the period of Ottoman rule as quickly as possible, as though nothing good can have come out of those years. "When at the end of the fourteenth century Bulgaria fell under Ottoman domination," asserted Todor Zhivkov in 1981, "the natural course of her historical development was stopped and reversed." Such a view predated Zhivkov's Communist regime and survives it too. The Serbian legend of the battle of Kosovo in 1389 reflects the same obsession with the question of legacy. Greek historians and preservationists are much more likely to work on ancient, Byzantine or modern history than on the Ottoman period. Historians of Britain do not, on the whole, spend much time wondering how much their country owes to its Anglo-Saxon, Norman or Hanoverian heritage; but questions of continuity, rupture and historical legacy are inescapable in the Balkans since what Halecki calls "the European point of view" has shaped many of the preoccupations of scholars and popular opinion in the region itself. And this is not because people there have some peculiar propensity to lose themselves in the mists of time, but rather because to be European has meant nothing less than denying the legitimacy of the Ottoman past. Reconstructing a respectable record of nationalist struggle and resistance against imperial oppression became necessary for membership of the European club. Nationalist passions and anxieties are, in other words, expressions of the effort to produce the kind of historical pedigree once—if not still—required by Europe itself.[23]

Because the Balkans have had a bad press for so long in Europe, it has been hard for some scholars to resist bringing out the region's virtues. National histories, until very recently, presented the past as the inevitable and entirely deserved triumph of the Nation over its enemies. More recently, a disillusionment with nationalism has bred nostalgia for the days of empire; a new trend in Ottoman historiography emphasizes ethnic and religious coexistence under the sultans and turns the empire into a kind of multicultural paradise *avant la lettre*. But the glossy version of Ottoman rule is not much of an improvement on the old negativity, except as a corrective to it. The truth is that while for many centuries religious coexistence was undoubtedly more accepted under the Ottomans than almost anywhere in Christendom, there was certainly no sense of religious equality. If there was no ethnic conflict, it was not because of "tolerance" but because there was no concept of nationality among the Sultan's subjects, and because Christianity stressed the "community of believers" rather than ethnic solidarity.[24]

Normative history sets up one pattern of historical evolution as standard and then explains deviations from that. The nineteenth-century mind took it for granted that history worked in this way, and that what one was describing was the success or failure of any given society in climbing the path of progress from backwardness and barbarism to civilization. In preferring to talk about the path from tradition to modernity, twentieth-century scholars have changed the terms but retained much of the same linear view. They have drawn on supposedly universal models of economic development and political democratization in order to understand why Balkan states and societies have remained poor and unstable and have not turned out as they should have done. But it is questionable whether relative poverty in southeastern Europe—or indeed the politics of ethnic violence—can really be explained as marks of backwardness. Since the ethnic mix of the Balkans has remained remarkably unchanged for centuries—during most of which there was no ethnic conflict at all—why is it only in the last one or two centuries that the cocktail became politically volatile? Contemporary contingencies of mass politics and urban, industrial life, the rise of new state structures and the spread of literacy and technology may well turn out to be as important in the Balkans as the supposed eternal verities of religious fracture, peasant rootedness and ethnic cleavage. We might find then that the story we tell does not so much affirm as undermine any sense of European superiority. For just as Europe gave the Balkans the categories with which its peoples defined themselves, so it gave them also the ideological weapons—in the shape primarily of modern romantic nationalism—with which to destroy themselves. Trying to understand the Balkans, in other words, challenges us to look at history itself as something more than a mirror which we hold up, blocking out the past to reflect our own virtues.

THE LAND AND ITS INHABITANTS

Mountains come first.

—FERNAND BRAUDEL[1]

Over millions of years, the play of the earth's tectonic plates pushed up a series of mountain ranges in the Mediterranean along the geological frontier between Europe and Africa. Stretching from the Iberian peninsula in the west to the ranges of southeastern Europe in the east, they eventually link up with the mountain chains of Asia Minor and central Asia. To their north, the great Eurasian lowlands extend with scarcely a break from Calais to the Urals. There rainfall is abundant, arable land is plentiful and numerous navigable rivers connect the interior with the sea. To the south, it is a different story: good farming land becomes scarcer, the ground is more broken and rainfall less frequent.

Unlike the mountain chains guarding the necks of the Iberian and Italian peninsulas, the Balkan ranges offer no barrier against invasion, leaving the region open to easy access and attack from north and east. On the other hand, their irregular formation hinders movement between one valley and the next. Communication is often easier with areas outside the peninsula than between its component parts, so that Dubrovnik, for instance, has had closer ties for much of its history with Venice than with Belgrade. In this way, mountains have made commerce within the region more expensive and complicated the process of political unification.

The effect of mountains is felt everywhere from the skies to the sea. Rain shadows deprive much of the peninsula of the moisture found in Europe's continental climatic zone. Kolašin in Montenegro has an average annual rainfall of 104 inches, while a little way east, Skopje in Macedonia has only 18 inches per year. A tiny coastal strip running down the Dalmatian coast to western Greece enjoys sufficient rain to soften the impact of the harsh Mediterranean summers. On Corfu the vegetation is luxuriant; the Cyclades, by contrast, are parched and dry. The former is able to support itself, the latter—as wartime starvation revealed—relies on food imports to keep going. In general, the annual precipitation east of the mountains is at least 10 to 20 inches less than farther west, leading to recurrent droughts even in the fertile plains. "A dreary arid sandy level" was how the Vardar valley presented itself to an intrepid Englishwoman crossing it in the mid-nineteenth century. "For many miles the country is entirely without trees."[2]

In the Mediterranean climatic zone, watercourses dry up during the summer, leaving rocky beds and canyons. The result is parched, broken upland with scarce water supplies—a harsh environment for human habitation that is suited chiefly to abstemious plants. "A curious feature in the mountains began to make itself painfully felt," noted Arthur Evans in 1875, walking across the Hercegovinan karst. "There was no water." He describes "a prospect of desolation.... In every direction rose low mountains, mere heaps of disintegrated limestone rock, bare of vegetation...aptly compared to a petrified glacier or a moonscape." Where summer rain permits, mountain forests and woodland—with beeches, oaks and sweet chestnuts—testify to perennial supplies of running water. Even so, the peninsula suffers drought more than anywhere else in Europe, except southern Spain and Malta, and deaths caused by water scarcity were reported from Montenegro as late as 1917.[3]

Not everywhere in the Balkans is as dry as this. In the Rhodope mountains, rivers flow throughout the year; the Albanian uplands remind travelers of Alpine meadows. Farther east, large parts of former Yugoslavia, Romania and northern Bulgaria enjoy something closer to a central European weather pattern. Long cool winters and heavy rains nourished the impenetrable *Shumadija*, which once covered much of lowland Serbia in dense oak forest. "Endless and endless now on either side the tall oaks closed over us," wrote Alexander Kinglake in *Eothen*, describing a ride toward Constantinople in 1834. "Through this our road was to last for more than a hundred miles."[4]

To the east, the Danube estuary shares climatic features with the southern steppes and the Black Sea, though it suffers from a lack of rainfall where the rain shadow of the Carpathians makes itself felt. Mountains make the contrast between Mediterranean and these northern and eastern weather zones a sudden one, as anyone who has climbed the road from Kotor on the Dalmatian coast to the old Montenegrin capital Cetinje will know. "The climate had suddenly changed," wrote a traveler after having traversed the Balkan mountains in Ottoman Bulgaria. "A warmer air surrounded us. The whole of European Turkey, from the southern declivities of the Haemus, lies in a delightful climate, which can display all the charms of the tropics as well as the vigor of the higher latitudes, without suffering their disagreeable effects."[5] For this sun-deprived northerner, not even the plague was enough to overshadow his sense of warmth and well-being as he came closer to the Mediterranean.

Rivers are generally crucial for prosperity because until modern times transportation was easier and cheaper by water than by land. Some historians explain the "European miracle" by the abundance of navigable waterways that connect coasts and the interior. But river systems that compare with the Rhine and Rhone in west Europe, or the Vistula–Dnieper trade route in east Europe, do not exist in the southeast of the continent. Balkan rivers, when more than winter torrents, descend too rapidly to be navigable, or else they meander idly in curves and loops away from the nearest coastline. Important rivers such as the Sava, the Vardar and the Aliákmon are thus of limited use for trade and communications. "Nothing can be more striking," wrote Henry Tozer in 1867 as he traveled south down the Vardar, "than the entire absence of towns along this great artery of internal communication.... The river itself is a fine sight when it flows in one stream, but...the work of making it navigable would now be a difficult one."[6] Even the Danube has served the region less well than it might, blocked from the Mediterranean by the mountains and then heading north—in quite the wrong direction from the merchant's point of view—before reaching the Black Sea. Before the Second World War, the lower Danube iced over for four to five months of the year. And before the early nineteenth century, while fought over by the Russians and the Turks, it was scarcely used for commerce at all; trade caravans between the Balkans and central Europe went by road, while travelers and diplomats en route to the Ottoman capital frequently left the river halfway along its course and completed their journey overland instead.

The same mountains that obstruct river passages to the sea precluded the construction of canals of the kind which helped commerce to flourish in eighteenth-century England and France. They also complicated the construction of railways. Rail moved across Europe like a frontier that replaced wooden towns with brick ones—in a slow and gradual movement from the north and west to the southeast of the continent. While the basic German network was in place by 1870, and had ramified to the Habsburg empire by the end of that decade, it was only after the late 1880s that key rail lines were laid south of the Danube. Both Habsburg and Ottoman authorities made a determined effort to modernize their Balkan domains, but political, strategic and topographical factors intervened and impeded rail construction. And while railways allowed goods to penetrate inland markets from the coastal areas, they did not help create a more unified or coherent regional economy. Rail networks themselves were less dense in the Balkans than anywhere else in Europe west of Brest Litovsk: 21.9 kilometers per thousand square kilometers in Greece in the 1920s, and 31.5 in the old prewar kingdom of Romania, compared with 97 in France, 123 in Germany and 370 in Belgium.[7]

Inheriting a rich network of paved interregional roads from the Romans, the Ottoman authorities developed an effective postal service using inns, caravanserais and post stations that allowed the Tartar government couriers to find fresh horses every few hours and a night's lodging where necessary. By the eighteenth century, however, this system faced collapse—there were delays and not enough horses—though it still worked well enough in 1841 to impress one traveler as "perhaps the only public service reasonably organized which exists in this country." By the mid-nineteenth century, the roads were so poor that some detected a deliberate policy by the Turkish authorities of keeping them in disrepair. "It is a favorite idea with all barbarous princes," asserted one writer, "that the badness of the roads adds considerably to the natural strength of their dominions." But mountain villagers had their own interest in bad roads too—they made it harder for the authorities to collect taxes. They made trade costlier as well. "Want of roads beyond the district makes exportation next to impossible" was one diagnosis why the fertile Monastir plain exported so little in the mid-nineteenth century. Bulgarian roads at the same time were in "a state of nature" and said to be "good enough in summer." Bessarabian roads were notorious as among the worst in Europe well into the 1930s. Before the improvements ordered by Serbian Prince Miloš Obrenović, the one hundred kilometers from Belgrade to Kragujevac took a week to travel.

From the middle of the nineteenth century onward, schemes of road improvement were pursued throughout the

Balkans; in the Ottoman domains, however, improvements initiated by one governor were often simply abandoned once he had been posted elsewhere; for want of upkeep, for instance, a new road laid near Serres in the 1860s was rendered impassable to wheeled transport in just five years. The Salonika Cycling Club, formed at the end of the nineteenth century, was unable to organize excursions beyond the city itself because the roads were so bad. The coming of the railways, which did form the object of Ottoman official concern, often resulted in reduced maintenance of local roads as goods and commerce shifted to the train.[8]

If well-kept roads had not been necessary to Ottoman patterns of conquest, it was largely thanks to the empire's comparative advantage over its competitors in beasts of burden—the water buffalo, mule, donkey and, above all, its special weapon, the camel, whose novelty and significance astonished contemporary observers. In 1684, the year after the Turks had been beaten back from the gates of Vienna, Johann Christoph Wagner included in his sweeping survey of the Ottoman domains a long eulogy of the virtues of this "splendidly useful" animal, which was "especially reputed" as "the best creation of God." "What shall I tell you of?" Lady Mary Wortley Montagu wrote a friend in 1717. "You never saw Camels in your Life and perhaps the Description of them will appear new to you." Rapid advances of the Ottoman armies, setting out from Edirne or Constantinople at the start of the campaigning season, relied especially upon these temperamental animals, capable of carrying huge loads over dirt roads, indifferent to mud and slower to tire or thirst than horses. "There are three hundred camels that carry weapons," noted Konstantin Mihailovic, who saw service in the Ottoman army in the late fifteenth century, "for they have no wagons, so that they will not be delayed with them when they march to war." For the acute Ogier Ghiselin de Busbecq, there were "two things from which, in my opinion, the Turks derive the greatest advantage and profit, rice among cereals and camels among beasts of burden; both are admirably adapted to the distant campaigns which they wage.... Camels can carry very heavy burdens, endure hunger and thirst, and require very little attention." Camels continued to be employed in the region well after the heroic age was over; near Delphi in 1884, Agnes Smith spied farmers using some—perhaps descendants of the animals plundered by Greek revolutionaries from Ottoman troops in the Peloponnese during the War of Independence six decades earlier. By the 1920s they had become a curiosity for tourists.[9]

By contrast, the horses that were used by merchants for the fifty-day journey from Macedonia to Vienna—caravans of as many as one thousand conveyed goods from the Balkans to central Europe well into the nineteenth century—fared poorly on the rough tracks and irregular, stony ground. The horses of Rustchuk, in Danubian Bulgaria, which were specially bred for the army cavalry in the early nineteenth century, were prized for their endurance on rocky terrain. But horses were costly to feed, water and look after. Down on the plains, buffaloes and oxen drew carts, plows and even carriages; while in the hills themselves, mules remained the pack animal of choice as late as the 1940s, when trains of hundreds of mules—their drivers fluent in the recently defunct language of the muleteer—carried German and British arms across the mountains of Yugoslavia and Greece during the war.

In what was always a border zone of Europe, the costs to any state of exerting its authority over the region were thus raised further by the character of the terrain itself. Insecurity was endemic for centuries and took its toll on economic life. In the summer of 1997, after an uprising in southern Albania, armed gangs held up cars across the Greek border and made travel at night unsafe even for the local police. They were the most recent chapter in a much older story; a century earlier, the Ottoman state had been unable to guarantee the safety of travelers after dark. In some areas, of course, it could not protect them during the day either. "The Pasha, who was concerned for our safety, would not listen to our passing the Balcan at Shumla, as robberies and assassinations had occurred there," wrote von Tietz in 1836, "but recommended us to go by Tirnovo which, although more inconvenient, was much more safe." By sea, travelers faced the threat of pirates between the fifteenth and early nineteenth centuries. Pirates remained a menace in the Aegean until they were stamped out by joint Ottoman–Greek action in 1839.[10]

The Ottoman state could cope with this state of affairs. It was used to negotiating with, and often amnestying and bringing into official service those outlaws, rebels and brigands too powerful or elusive to punish and kill. Only with the rise of the modern state in the nineteenth and twentieth century—an entity defined in part by its insistence on preserving a monopoly of the use of armed force, and in part by the extent of its ambition to control its own population—were these challengers to its prestige sought out and hunted down. When a brigand band looted Sámos in 1925 and held the island's capital for several days, the newspapers in Athens were loud in condemnation: "We should not spare any sacrifice, any means in order to eliminate by radical means the architects of acts which dishonor the country and provoke greater harm to its progress," wrote one. "The State has not only the duty but also the highest interest to put a stop, without the slightest delay, to these misfortunes...and to show that its power stands above every individual and everything." Modern policing, bureaucracies and roads altered the balance of power in favor of the central authorities; as a result, brigandage and piracy ceased in the twentieth century to plague commerce and travel. Only brief periods of acute destabilization—in the 1940s and 1990s—called up pale echoes of what had once been a chronic social problem.[11]

—

Push population figures very far back into history and you quickly come up with hypotheses rather than facts. Absolute numbers for populations anywhere in the world before the eighteenth century are largely a matter of guesswork. Even for the nineteenth century, estimates of the size, say, of the Bulgarian population have ranged from 500,000 to 8 million. On the one hand, Balkan statistics have long been manipulated for political purposes; on the other, official Ottoman figures were not designed for modern scholarly purposes. Even so, the long-run demographic trends in the Balkans are fairly clear. For much of its history, the southeast of Europe was a wilderness with large quantities of uncultivated land and relatively few people, especially in the lowlands. Depopulation probably occurred as a consequence of chronic political instability in the final stages of the Byzantine empire, and was evidently not remedied by the Ottoman efforts to resettle the Balkans with nomadic Turkic colonists. Population densities in 1600, when the Ottoman empire was flourishing, were still perhaps half those of France or Italy, and one third those of the Low Countries, though they were far higher than in the Ottoman domains in Asia. "The whole country from Ragusa [Dubrovnik] until within a few miles of Constantinople is for the most part uncultivated and horrible" noted Benedetto Ramberti, the Venetian ambassador to the Porte, "not by nature but by the negligence of the inhabitants, full of dangerous forests and terrible precipices, very unsafe on account of brigands, very wretched as to accommodation." "In the Ottomans' estate," wrote William Lithgow in 1632, "there be great Forrests, and desartuous Countries, proceeding of the scarcity of people to inhabit there."[12]

Still, population rose and fell in the peninsula apace with the European average until the seventeenth century. Not only did the Ottoman conquest in the fifteenth century *not* interrupt this trend, the sixteenth century was evidently a time of prosperity and high population growth in the Balkans, as elsewhere in Europe. Evidence from local studies indicates that even Christians who had fled the invading Turks returned from Venetian domains to reclaim their properties.[13]

The real crisis came later in the seventeenth century. Times were hard everywhere in Europe, but in the southeast they were disastrously affected by a combination of political instability, endless wars, frequent plagues and famine. Plague in particular could cut a city's population by half or even more, and the Balkans were vulnerably located on the disease routes from the Near East to western Europe; some cities were afflicted almost every year. "The sickness rageth as if it would dispeople the citty," noted Sir Thomas Roe in 1625 as he fled Constantinople. He estimated that the death toll was more than 1,000 daily at its height, and "neare 200,000" in all. In the plagues of 1781–1783, more than 300 a day died in Salonika—"reduced almost to a desert," in the words of the Venetian consul there—while 16,000 died in Sarajevo. Visitations of the plague varied enormously in the number of their victims—not all had such catastrophic consequences—just as they did in the rest of Europe. London and Marseilles were also struck down by plague in the seventeenth century—Marseilles may have lost half its inhabitants in 1720. The difference was that by the start of the eighteenth century, most of western and central Europe had strict and effective quarantine measures in place (often applied against travelers from Ottoman domains)—indeed, control and management of contagious diseases were a major stimulus to the emergence of the modern bureaucratic state; in the Levant, by contrast, plagues recurred for another century and a half, and the last great epidemic struck as late as the years 1835–1838.[14]

Overall figures are unreliable but the trend is clear. Only at the beginning of the nineteenth century did the population of the Balkans begin to approach again the level it had reached in the late sixteenth century and start to move consistently upward. By 1831, at the time of the first Ottoman census, it was probably around 10 million—or just under 20 million when including the populations of Serbia and the future Croatia and Romania. Once the Balkan states won independence, their population began increasing very fast. By the beginning of the twentieth century, the old Ottoman problem of underpopulation had been replaced by the historically new pressure of high birth rates and falling death rates. In 1920 the population of the Balkans was roughly 42.5 million, and rising faster than anywhere else in Europe. "The cardinal facts," according to one report of 1940, "are that [the Balkan states] are agricultural, overpopulated and poor."[15]

This demographic pressure on the land was unprecedented. Even at the start of the nineteenth century, a British visitor to Wallachia was impressed by the "incredible richness of the soil"—grass came up to his elbow, the weeds were as tall as a man—and noted "the trifling population of Wallachia (about a million), which is not the tenth part of what the soil could nourish." With independence, population densities rapidly increased—from 181 inhabitants per square kilometer in Serbia in 1834 to 55.7 in 1905, from 11.8 to 36.1 in Moldavia between 1803 and 1859. Major shifts in patterns of settlement and land use ensued.[16]

As human numbers rocketed, the number of sheep shrank and shepherding fell into decline. Brigandage (in the nineteenth century) and emigration (in the twentieth) were two responses to this demographic dilemma. "The inhabitants live by agriculture or in bad season brigandage, though of late the younger men have begun to emigrate to America," wrote two British travelers to western Macedonia in 1910–1911. Quitting the countryside to look for work in the towns or specializing in cash crops were other options. But between the two world wars, the state stamped out brigandage (or tried to), the United States curtailed immigration and the economic depression made cash crops unprofitable. Only after the Second World War were solutions to Balkan "underemployment" found through rapid economic growth, renewed emigration and industrialization. After 1960, prosperity pushed birth rates down toward the European average in all but the poorest parts of the peninsula. In other words, the emergence in the Balkans of urban populations at a level close to the European norm, with its characteristic pattern of small families, high consumption, industry and services, is entirely a product of the last five or six generations. Until well into this century, the peasantry predominated, for few people lived in the towns, and few of those who did lacked close ties to the land.[17]

———

Looking at the peasants dressed in their picturesque costumes, foreign visitors were struck by the persistence of what they regarded as an antiquated life form. "In most ways the native seems to have changed little since Biblical days," wrote two British students of Macedonia in 1921, "so that it may almost be said that in observing the modern Macedonian one is studying the type amongst whom St. Paul preached and traveled." Their view that "the primitiveness of the native peasantry is their most marked feature" was one shared implicitly both by travel writers and by postwar modernization theorists and social anthropologists. Ethnographers, enthralled by the nineteenth-century romantic view of peasants as the repository of national tradition, charted what they took to be the pagan origins of their beliefs, ornaments and customs; American classicists heard in the oral epic poetry of Serbian *guslar* players the direct descendants of Homer. It is as though the emergence of the idea of modernity in nineteenth-century Europe, with its sharp sense of time moving ahead fast, encouraged a view of the Balkans as a place where "time has stood still."[18]

Many farming and food technologies, it is true, changed little over time. The Bulgarian peasant huts made of plaited branches covered with foliage that Robert de Dreux saw outside Serres in the late seventeenth century can have scarcely differed from those of a thousand years earlier. Even more elementary were the hovels inhabited by nineteenth-century Romanian peasants: "the *ne plus ultra* of disgusting dirtiness and wretchedness," wrote a traveler, "consisting of holes dug in the earth, over which a propped roof is thrown—covered rarely with straw, generally with turf." Peasant tools—the wooden plows and cart wheels, the stone pestles—were slower to alter than elsewhere in Europe, as was a sense of time marked not by hours and minutes but by the passage of the sun and the saints' days. Orthodox Christians regarded Catholic Europe's move to the Gregorian calendar as an unacceptable innovation. The introduction of public clocks lagged behind the rest of the continent; as late as 1868 there were none in Montenegro.[19]

Yet the primitive, eternally unchanging peasant was a figment of the Western romantic imagination. Despite the large and ever growing gap that separated them from west European commercial farming, Balkan peasants were capable of rapid adaptation, movement and change. Their history is one not of stasis but of innovation and experimentation with new crops (as with corn, tobacco, citrus fruits, the potato and the tomato). In the mid-nineteenth century, when official dress codes lost their legal character, it was townspeople who began first to wear the new "Frankish" outfits, and the peasantry who remained faithful longest to the older distinctive costumes; yet they too changed, and umbrellas, sewing machines and black stockings infiltrated the most remote mountain passes faster than the Ottoman gendarmerie.

Far from being rooted to the spot, farming men and women often migrated surprising distances, whether to pasture herds, to look for seasonal work as inn hands or road builders, or as stonemasons and carpenters. Bulgarian peasant men, armed with two weeks' supply of home-baked bread, were harvesting the wheat fields of central Europe in the 1920s. Baron Sina, one of the richest men in Habsburg Vienna, was the scion of Vlach villagers from the Pindos who had emigrated northward. Entire villages might relocate themselves in response to political, environmental or economic changes—border changes, natural catastrophes (such as drought) or abrupt fluctuations in crop prices were enough to prompt mass migration. Settlements would be moved up a mountain slope to get away from danger by sea or road, and then moved back down again as life became more secure. And some basic peasant institutions such as the Slavic *zadruga* (a form of collectivity that combined three or four related families as a single living and working unit) which earlier scholars assumed were of great antiquity (perhaps because they are inclined to assume that the family itself is an institution which changes little in rural society), turn out to have been relatively recent innovations. In short, even though the farming smallholder remained the mainstay of the Balkan world for more than a millennium—outlasting the Byzantine and Ottoman empires—he and his family did not do this by standing still. And ironically it was just when Westerners were discovering these living fossils—in the last two hundred years—that peasants were changing the most to meet the challenges of capitalism and cash production.[20]

The coming of the Turks is often seen as ushering in a new dark age from which Balkan Christians never fully recovered. In fact, Ottoman rule probably benefited the peasantry. For more than two hundred years they had suffered from the political instability of the late Byzantine world and infighting among their lords and masters. Christian landowners—Greek, Slav, French, Venetian and Catalan—had ruled over them with increasing harshness in the preceding centuries; it was this domineering class that Ottoman conquest swept away. Only in the Danubian Principalities (and in parts of Bosnia) did an indigenous landowning class survive—thanks to more indirect Ottoman rule—with the result that through into the twentieth century peasants there were more harshly exploited than anywhere else in southeast Europe. Everywhere else, the Balkan peasant found his old oppressor gone (thanks to the Turks) and a freedom of movement (thanks to the mountains) denied to the serfs of Prussia, Hungary and Russia. Centuries later, when the Balkan states won independence they would be "peasant democracies," with no aristocracy of their own, a fundamentally different form of society from that found almost everywhere in Europe.[21]

Of course, new masters replaced the old. Ottoman soldiers (both Muslim and Christian) were rewarded with estates, and some of the old Byzantine labor duties were kept in force. Greek and Serbian notable families converted to Islam and moved into the Ottoman elite; a few, for a time, held on to their estates without converting. But the crucial break with the past was legal: under the regime instituted by the new empire, almost all arable land belonged to the ruler. In the words of an Ottoman document: "The land which was in the hands of the *reaya* [peasantry] at the time of the conquest was settled upon them once more with the ownership held in trust for the Muslim community."[22]

In the classical Ottoman model the central state, through its courts and bureaucracy, monitored and regulated relations between peasant and master. Unable easily to pass on their possessions to their heirs, the new estate holders never formed an aristocratic class capable of threatening the power of the ruling dynasty. They oppressed their peasant farmers, but never owned them; what they owned was the right to their produce. Moreover, they were registered by the state as ruthlessly and effectively as their peasants were. Overall tax burdens on farmers were probably no higher than before the Ottomans came. And the peasants themselves enjoyed more control over their lives than their counterparts in most of Europe. The almost endless wars that had ravaged parts of the Balkans in the fourteenth century were replaced by the stability brought by an organized imperial state pursuing a deliberate policy of repopulation. In the first century after the conquest, there was an increase in the area under cultivation. The spread of what we might call politically sensitive crops such as oranges, tomatoes, mulberries and later cotton and apricots—all of which require investment in expensive irrigation systems—is one indicator of stability on the land. So too is the rapid growth in the population of Constantinople (and other, smaller cities), which depended on a healthy agricultural economy for its sustenance.[23]

After two to three centuries of Ottoman rule, however, the empire began to confront new difficulties, facing tougher military opposition as it expanded and finding it harder and harder to raise the tax revenues to pay for incessant wars. Compared with other European powers—France, Spain, even Venice—Ottoman methods of tax farming hindered rather than promoted expansion. Western European economies moved in the direction of new commercial banking, colonial trade, the promotion of private property and manufacturing growth. Some provincial elites in the

Ottoman empire did also emerge as private entrepreneurs, but the old economy continued to regulate the trade and production of most major commodities and discouraged private investment. To this stuttering Leviathan the Balkans were indispensable, since they provided roughly two thirds of the tax revenues of the entire empire. The bulk of these was paid by the peasantry.

In the writings of an eighteenth-century Ottoman official, Sari Mehmed Pacha, we see the bureaucracy's traditional argument for treating the peasants well and keeping an eye on the provincial beys. "Let them neither oppress the poor *rayahs* [peasants]," he states, "nor cause them to be vexed by the demand for new impositions in addition to the well-known yearly taxes which they are accustomed to give. All the experienced sages have likened the taking for inessential expenditures of more money than they can endure from the *rayahs* to taking from the foundation of a building and transferring it to the roof.... Such being the case, the poor peasants should not be troubled by any sort of evil innovation."[24]

Yet on the land a major innovation was taking place: a new provincial elite—mostly Muslim, but including some Christian notables—was emerging, which owned villages and fields and passed these possessions on to the next generation. The older Ottoman land regime was passing away and being replaced by one in which privately owned estates encroached on former common lands and dispossessed the peasants. The causes of the rise of these *chiflik* estates—their nature and extent—is among the most bitterly contested issues in Ottoman historiography. Whether these estates were a response, as was once thought, to growing commercial opportunities in the international economy or, as now seems more likely, to the growing political power of a more exploitative class of tax-farming landlords, the outcome was a deterioration in the condition of the peasantry.[25]

Balkan peasants, however, were still more fortunate than the enserfed farmhands of the central and east European flatlands. Many villages preserved their autonomy under the leadership of local notables, who collected the taxes and had their own interest in keeping the peasants' fiscal burden bearable. For if it became too oppressive, the peasants fled in growing numbers from the plains to towns, to lands outside the region and, above all, to the hills. Entire villages were abandoned once those who had initially chosen to remain realized they were still liable for the taxes of those who had already departed. At the same time, the introduction and rapid spread of corn cultivation had in J. R. McNeill's words "a revolutionary effect on the mountains," as it allowed upland villages to support more people than in the past. Family and clan farming guaranteed the necessary hands for clearing woodland and tilling small upland plots. Females cost dowries to marry off but were reckoned to be able to carry half the load of a donkey, and provided cheap pack labor. Their bodies often reflected their arduous social position. "Women are early worn out," Edith Durham noted. "Especially in Montenegro there is a very great difference in height between men and women. Women I found were usually shorter than I am [five foot three inches]; whereas men well over six foot are not uncommon."[26]

Safe from pirates, malaria, plagues, tax collectors and marauding militias, hill people were able to negotiate more advantageous tax terms with the imperial government. In remote regions such as the Agrafa (i.e., "the unregistered lands"), the Albanian uplands and Montenegro, autonomous—indeed virtually free—peasant communities were able more or less to disregard their nominal masters. "They pay an annual tribute," wrote Dmitry Kantemir of the Moldavian mountain "republic" near Suceava in the early eighteenth century. "If the prince decides to beat them harshly they do not spend time in negotiating but refuse the tribute altogether and retire to the more inaccessible parts of the mountains. For this reason the princes never ask them for more than their due." Other villages won tax exemptions by agreeing to serve as "pass defenders" against brigands, guaranteeing security of passage. In August 1715, after a successful summer campaign against the Venetians in the Peloponnese, the Grand Vezir Ali Pasha negotiated over this issue with a delegation of Greeks from the mountainous Mani peninsula, whose villages "form a kind of Republic," according to the campaign's chronicler.[27]

Yet political autonomy came at the price of a constant struggle to make a living. In the nineteenth century, mountain communities started for the first time to face overpopulation. Their basic diet was healthy, and on average people grew taller than in the plains. But the parched mountains did not generate enough food to last the year round—at Metsovo, the local harvest was reckoned to be good for barely one or two months—forcing their inhabitants to find other supplementary livelihoods. Forests provided berries and mushrooms for picking (another skill now dying out), charcoal and timber for sale. Hill villagers also sold snow to the lowlands; as late as the 1920s—before the advent of mass refrigeration—snow was being sold in Jannina, and was still profitable despite a 65 percent meltage rate. They needed something to sell in order to buy the salt from the lowlands that alone made life possible in these food-deficit communities.

Brigandage offered a more "heroic" way of making money. The typical mid-nineteenth-century bandit, according to the author of an illuminating study of the phenomenon, was "a young mountaineer, between twenty and thirty years old or younger, and, more often than not, a migratory shepherd." Pushed outside the law, often by his own violent actions, the brigand's primary purpose was usually to secure an amnesty and if possible an official appointment in the service of the state as local watchman. In the meantime, he talked tough and tried to make himself as intimidating as possible. "Your coffee is ours, your money is ours, and your blood is ours," one Albanian brigand reminded his British captive. "Everyone is in debt to the robber. I am sultan here; I am king of England here."[28]

Robbers and sheep stealers were a growing problem in the eighteenth and nineteenth centuries. As the Ottoman empire shrank and disintegrated, frontiers proliferated across which brigands could roam, fleeing pursuers and often enjoying political protection in neighboring states as self-proclaimed patriots. In reality, they were as likely to prey on poor Christian farmers as on Muslims, often taking the self-serving and self-righteous line that Christians who remained under Turkish rule were no better than Turks themselves. "Great alarm prevailed in all directions respecting the robbers," noted the intrepid David Urquhart traveling to Mount Athos in the 1830s. "They had been guilty of fearful atrocities, and had, by attacking on several occasions the peasantry, aroused the feelings of the people against them." These brigands were neither social bandits—robbing the rich to aid the poor—nor national heroes; rather, they were a symptom of high-altitude poverty and one way of trying to ameliorate it. Their sense of honor was highly developed; raiding sheep or cattle was considered a more heroic pursuit than conventional and sedentary ways of earning a living. Yet the brigand's lot, stripped of the mystique, was a miserable one. The Greek chief of the band that seized Urquhart tried to excuse himself to his captive: "Look at those men, some of them barefoot, with clothes of string rather than cloth, with empty tobacco bags, and empty stomachs; what makes them lead such a life, and what restraint can you place on men who live so . . . driven like oxen in the fields, or hunted like bears in the mountains?"[29]

Alongside the brigands—putting up with them, suffering from them and sometimes joining them—were the shepherds whose way of life had profited most from the collapse of settled farming in the plains. Between the seventeenth and the early twentieth centuries was the golden age of the pastoral economy in the Balkans. Military men, according to a 1609 document from Rumelia, were taking over abandoned holdings, settling slaves on them and converting the properties to livestock grazing. With their huge flocks of sheep, the shepherds wintered in the valleys on St. Dimitrios's Day (November 8) and moved camp again on St. George's Day (May 6) to spend the summers on mountain pasture, often traveling hundreds of miles in the process. The fact that their taxes had to be paid in cash made shepherds familiar with the demands of a money economy. They sold their livestock, sheepskins, woolen goods and cheeses in village markets or at the great annual fairs that were the motors of Balkan commerce until the early twentieth century. Gradually some settled as merchants: a small hill town like Metsovo high in the Pindos was in fact surprisingly wealthy by the middle of the nineteenth century thanks to the business ventures of these men.[30]

Occasionally hill settlements enjoyed the right mix of seclusion, water and raw materials to permit what economic historians call proto-industrialization. "The villages which are least favored in respect of soil," wrote Leake, "have resources in the manufacture of cotton and wool....It is reckoned that one third of the inhabitants of Agrafa gain a living by weaving. There are also many workers in gold and silver; and at Skatina is a fabric of swords-blades, gun barrels and locks of pistols." Textile production in small factories in Greek and especially Bulgarian upland settlements spread in the decades before these regions won independence. But by the early nineteenth century, competition from Western imports was hitting them hard, and previously prosperous mountain manufacturers such as Ambelakia fell on hard times. Thereafter, such activities—where they survived— descended to the towns and cities.[31]

The coming of Ottoman rule had perhaps a greater impact upon the town dweller than on the peasant. Where a town surrendered without a fight during the period of conquest, the Porte usually refrained from sacking it. Nevertheless, many Byzantine towns from the capital downward were ruined and devastated by the conquerors. But the Ottomans knew that towns were vital for the administration of the empire; for Mehmed the Conqueror, their renewal was the "mightiest war" compared with which military victory had been merely the "lesser war." The Ottomans quickly repopulated major urban centers like Constantinople through the forced resettlement of Christians, Jews and Muslims. For similar reasons, Sultan Bayezid II welcomed Sephardic Jews expelled from Spain, Portugal and southern Italy in the late fifteenth century, and prominent Sephardic communities took root in the towns of the empire.[32]

By the end of the fifteenth century, the Porte had made a determined effort to revivify urban life. High court officials were encouraged to finance complexes of public buildings— caravanserais, covered markets, public baths, mosques and schools, hospitals, aqueducts—in order to provide the services required by an urban population. Many former Byzantine cities—notably, the capital—recovered their strength, while a number of new settlements emerged, including Bosna Seraj (Sarajevo), Banja Luka and Mostar in Bosnia, Tirana (the future capital of Albania) and smaller towns such as Elbasan and Yannitsa. The population of these towns was often overwhelmingly Muslim, while the countryside remained largely Christian. According to the tax registers of 1520–1530, more than 80 percent of the inhabitants of the Balkans were Christians. Yet Muslims outnumbered Christians in most major Balkan urban settlements.[33]

Historians are divided as to whether the overall impact of Ottoman rule marked a disjuncture or a continuation of city life. One thing is clear, however: there was no overall decline. It was only under the sultans that walled fortresses such as Belgrade developed into larger commercial and administrative centers with extensive suburbs. Major urban projects, such as large mosques, were completed rapidly by European standards, testifying to the empire's ability to mobilize labor effectively even in small market towns such as Serres and Prizren. Overall, the degree of urbanization in the Balkans increased in the early phases of Ottoman rule, and coastal trading cities such as Salonika and Dubrovnik (effectively an Ottoman vassal) prospered. By 1600, Constantinople was the largest city in Europe; even if we accept a low estimate of 250,000 inhabitants, it still overshadowed London (200,000), Paris (220,000) and Rome (105,000). Berlin (25,000), Madrid and Vienna (both 50,000) were unremarkable towns of the middling rank. Cairo, on the other hand, was bigger even than the imperial capital: "the most admirable and greatest City seene upon the earth," according to William Lithgow, who could compare it with most of its rivals. As for Edirne, the occasional seat of the Ottoman court, Lady Mary Wortley Montagu who visited it in 1717 and was not overly impressed, nonetheless admitted to "365 shops furnish'd with all sorts of rich Goods expos'd to sale in the same manner as at the New Exchange in London, but the pavements kept much neater, and the shops all so clean they seem'd just new painted. Idle people of all sorts walk here for their Diversion or amuse themselves with drinking coffee or sherbet." These were staples of Ottoman urban life before they were implanted into the cities of Western Europe.[34]

Towns were favored precisely because they were indispensable to the government of the empire. They were centers of administration from which the state could collect taxes, supervise trade and extract its monopoly of vital commodities such as salt. They existed in the shadow of Constantinople, which they fed through the food purchase quotas and elaborate provisioning system that lay at the heart of the Ottoman empire. Even after the central Ottoman state weakened in the course of the seventeenth century, the barriers to private capital accumulation on a West European model remained high. Trade and hence capital was gradually passing from Muslims and Jews into the hands of Christian Orthodox merchants, who did constitute an incipient bourgeoisie of sorts. But the latter were well aware of their vulnerability in the empire, and made sure that affiliates existed beyond its reach—in Vienna, Odessa or Marseilles—whither funds could be safely transferred. The cities themselves remained chiefly centers of commerce and handicrafts. They were also acutely prone to plague, suffering from what T. Stoianovich calls "exceptional pestilences," on an average of once every dozen years throughout the seventeenth and eighteenth centuries. And because the slow movement of the brick/stone frontier from northern to southeast Europe meant that houses were still mostly built of wood, fires devastated towns as late as the early twentieth century.[35]

By the early nineteenth century, it was the silence of Turkish towns that struck the Western visitor—the lack of church bells, the absence of wheeled vehicles and horseshoes, all of which testified to the lack of blacksmiths, metalworkers and machinery. "Amid the novelties that strike the European on his arrival," wrote William Turner in 1812, "nothing surprises him more than the silence that pervades so large a capital." If no real industrialization took place in towns under Ottoman rule, it was for the same reasons that commercial agriculture also made little progress in the empire: the lack of well-kept, well-secured roads; bureaucratic obstruction; religious objections to the spread of printed media and scientific knowledge; and levels of public disorder that, if anything, probably increased over time as the political struggle for Macedonia intensified. Lack of security for the rural population was a long-standing problem. "All the territory of the Gran Signor is dispeopled for want of justice, or rather by violent oppressions," Sir Thomas Roe had noted in 1622. But the problem did not disappear. Romania in the 1840s had "estates of monstrous size almost completely devoid of inhabitants." Having heard from Greeks in one lowland village how they were abused by the Turkish authorities, one British visitor understood better the rudimentary security system they had adopted. "We found the dogs very troublesome," wrote Captain J. J. Best in 1842. "No wonder they keep such fierce dogs when the inhabitants are liable to such treatment." But dogs were little use against the tax collector. "The first act of a Greek Bishop," wrote a local observer, "after his arrival at his post, is plunder." Tax farmers and moneylenders exploited the peasants' vulnerability to fluctuations in the harvest and their helplessness in the face of armed force. "The Wallachian is idle," wrote an observer of the Romanian lands, "because he knows he could not enjoy the fruits of industry, since they would be extorted from him under the name of tithes." The ensuing depopulation led to the abandonment of land, extensive farming and the use of arable land for pasture. Deforestation—a consequence of population strain up in the hills—accelerated soil erosion, the silting up of alluvial valleys and the spread of malaria.[36]

This depressing picture did not apply everywhere, to be sure. In the valley of the Morava, there were "rich crops of Indian corn...under good cultivation, and...a smooth expanse of fertile fields." In the eighteenth and nineteenth centuries, the large landowners who had begun to amass land included a few "improving" provincial rulers and notables. Ali Pasha of Jannina introduced silkworms, mulberries and rice cultivation into his domains. Before he was toppled by the Sultan, he "proceeded with the greatest severity" against the large bands of robbers who had infested his lands and "by opening the country to merchants and securing their persons and goods, has not only increased his own revenues, but bettered the condition of his subjects." The Bushatlis, another Albanian notable family of the eighteenth century, cultivated rice and cotton in their domains, which they exported to Italy; around Serres as well, cotton cultivation spread very fast. Some reforming Ottoman civil servants also sought to modernize the countryside and the towns. Midhat Pasha, who was probably the greatest Ottoman civil servant of the nineteenth century and was called Giaour Pasha by the Turks for his supposed partiality to the Christians, increased tax revenues and boosted agricultural production in Danubian Bulgaria. But Midhat Pasha did not last long, falling victim to the political insecurity that soon undid his work.

If the Ottoman lands never felt the full impact of improving landowners of the kind found in Western and central Europe, they could not escape the growing impact of Western capitalism, especially as trade linked the empire with markets in central Europe, France and farther afield. As the crisis of government deepened, the need for urgent reforms, intermittently tried since the early eighteenth century, became obvious to the Porte. For nearly a century, the power of the Sultan's household had been undermined by its inability to control the janissary corps, the court militia that had once been an integral part of the Ottoman machinery of conquest. Over time the janissaries evolved from an elite, loyal military cohort into a badly paid, independent and unruly interest group that on occasion even deposed sultans. By the eighteenth century, their defense of their privileges posed a far greater threat to the empire's own inhabitants than the corps did to its enemies. They were feared by their Christian neighbors, whom they attacked with impunity in the streets, by their fellow Muslims and by the Porte itself. After the defeat of Napoleon and the rise of the breakaway Mehmet Ali in Egypt, the central Ottoman state reasserted its authority in a bid to modernize its military and restore its own prestige: in 1826 the janissary corps in the capital was massacred and replaced by a professional army. Shortly afterward, British pressure compelled the Porte to liberalize trade and to promise equality before the law for all subjects of the empire. In the 1850s it finally became possible—at least in theory—to buy and sell land (a change not very much later, it should be noted, than that occurring in the Hungarian countryside). All this meant a weakening of the old intrusive regulatory imperial economy and permitted the expansion of commercial agriculture—cotton and tobacco, Serbian pigs and Romanian wheat—within an international market. Foreign capital, goods and investors followed.

Most peasants remained self-sufficient and mistrustful of money—with good reason, since they were probably worse off for capitalism's triumph. They faced now a centralized imperial state that was trying to collect taxes more efficiently, giving more legal power to landlords and whittling away customary peasant rights to land and produce. Capitalism was forcing change upon the Ottoman empire—the most threatening solvent of that sense of customary fairness that underpinned the Balkan peasantry's sense of the natural order. Over time, this led peasants toward what Stoianovich concisely describes as "a strategy of demanding the abolition both of the landlords and of the state that refused to abolish the landlords." Capitalism, in other words, and the modernization of the Ottoman state had political consequences. In the Turkish empire—as in Austria-Hungary and Tsarist Russia—the coming of a money economy and the modern state disrupted older patterns of social relations and helped pave the way for political changes as well.[37]

Only in the light of this dramatic economic and societal disruption can one understand the emergence of mass nationalism in the nineteenth-century Balkans. Nationalism as a mass movement inevitably involved the peasants, yet for them what counted was not the Nation or other abstract political concepts, but their rights to land, livelihood and fair taxes. As farming was monetized and traditional dues were replaced by cash obligations, class tensions increased in the countryside. The 1875 Hercegovina revolt, which triggered off a major collapse of Ottoman power in the Balkans, was provoked by harvest failure and the subsequent maltreatment of peasants by soldiers accompanying the tax farmers. It began, wrote the French consul in Sarajevo, "with protests of subjects of all religions against excessive tax demands." Another eyewitness was even clearer: "It is mainly an agrarian war...in its origin Agrarian rather than Political." Class antagonism and nationalism emerged together.[38]

The peasants were basically right: political independence favored them by creating conditions of relative tranquillity and security of property. Independence ended neither population pressure on land nor brigandage; indeed, both persisted for decades into the life of independent Greece, Montenegro and Serbia, often to the public embarrassment of the new states' leaders. But it did increase the overall security of the Christian majority, with immediate results. In 1841 Adolphe Blanqui had correctly predicted that "when Bulgaria enjoys a regime of security, the immense regions which today are left to the ravages of goats and poor pasturage will be put under cultivation." Crossing from the Ottoman lands into semi-independent Serbia in 1853, one traveler, who was not unsympathetic to the Turks, was struck that "we seemed to enter a new clime: the whole valley teemed with luxuriant crops, the road had been formed with care...and everything betokened industry and comfort, the result of security." As a result, after independence, hill dwellers descended again into the plains, population grew quickly and soon the margin of uncultivated land shrank.[39]

The newly enfranchised peasantry, possessed as if "by an insatiable desire for land," now cut back the ancient forests and extended their own holdings. "During the last decade, a frightful extent of woodland has been cleared," wrote a German visitor to Romania in 1900. The great forests of the Serbian Shumadija disappeared in a few decades. The shepherding economy, which had flourished for the past three hundred years, was plunged into crisis as pasture came under cultivation and governments carved up landed estates and distributed them to peasant smallholders. The Balkan land reforms of the 1920s, followed by a second wave after 1945 in those countries ruled by Communist parties, parceled up large tracts of land among the farmers of cash crops and deprived sheep of their traditional winter grazing grounds. New political borders severed summer from winter grazings. The transhumant shepherds became a vanishing breed, rare already in the 1950s, and today all but extinct. "Before 1922 it was not exceptional for a man to own 2,000 sheep," wrote a British anthropologist in 1964. "Today a flock of 500 is considerable."[40]

Thus, independence brought new difficulties to those who worked the land. "Land is becoming a commodity," noted a Croatian scholar of peasant life in 1935. Peasants were inexorably and often reluctantly drawn into the cash nexus, but on terms that left them less and less equipped to avoid debt. They parceled out holdings among their heirs so that within a few generations farmland was hopelessly fragmented and inefficient. High population growth accelerated this creation of a pattern of tiny, unviable plots. To make matters worse, the old patterns of collective farming, especially strong among the Slavs, began to disappear; the *zadruga* broke up as each family set up on its own. Atomization made the farmer less self-reliant and more dependent on farming for money. But there were few crops that allowed a peasant family any measure of prosperity for more than a generation or two. Those products—like tobacco or currants, Serbian plums and pigs—grown for export were exposed to the whims of the international market. In independent Romania, which had become one of the world's chief exporters of grain at the turn of the century, social tensions in the countryside—between the miserably impoverished peasant sharecroppers and the often Jewish merchants who leased the Moldavian estates—exploded in a peasant revolt in 1907. The worst peasant uprising in modern Balkan history was suppressed by the Romanian army only at the cost of an estimated eleven thousand lives. Romania had the least equal pattern of landholding in the Balkans—1 percent of landowners held nearly 50 percent of the arable and grazing lands, while perhaps 85 percent of peasant cultivators were operating at or below subsistence level. But the pressure of high reproduction rates and the fragmentation of landholdings was impoverishing other Balkan farming populations too.[41]

Mass emigration, especially overseas, demonstrated how hard the newly independent states were finding it to make peasant farming work. The portraits of Montenegrin, Croatian, Greek and Romanian Jewish country folk stare down at visitors to the Ellis Island Museum in New York, testifying to the great wave of immigrants to America from the Balkans. Migration had begun to gather pace in the last decades of Ottoman rule, but continued thereafter. By 1912, 250,000

Greeks had left for the United States, nearly 10 percent of the population and the largest proportion from any European state after 1900. Entire villages became dependent on remittances from overseas. Some areas started to suffer from labor shortages before the First World War, then U.S. immigration restrictions cut off the outflow. In the 1950s, the same pattern would emerge as Greek and Yugoslav peasants again fled the land for Australia and Germany: the land simply could not support the highest reproduction rates in Europe.

Peasants tried to resist the incursions of modernity. Their generosity and hospitality toward travelers—often codified into custom—existed alongside a deep suspicion of neighbors and the inhabitants of the next village, not to mention landlords. The hatred that existed between hill and valley was well known. "I'd rather marry a Turk than have to go around in black and wear a kerchief," was how sophisticated Dalmatian lowland girls mocked the highland shepherds who came to market in the early seventeenth century. "The plains were always held by someone alien to the mountaineers, who were hungry for bread and land, and tired of the bare, though beautiful crags that were their home," wrote the Montenegrin Milovan Djilas. In his memoirs, Djilas vividly conveys the mutual bitterness felt between peasant and town folk. "If the townspeople, erstwhile peasants, had contempt for the peasants," he writes, "the peasants in turn hated them.... The peasants looked down upon the townspeople as a sluggish, wily, and lying breed, who ate little and delicately, fancy soups, tripes and pastries—and wasted away in damp, crowded, little rooms."[42]

For centuries, the village had been the main political, administrative, fiscal and military unit organizing the collective lives of rural inhabitants of the Balkans. It was the village which they referred to as their "fatherland" and its representatives spoke for them before the dignitaries of the state and

other intruders. In the nineteenth century, this isolated collectivity began to change in ways its inhabitants found hard to
comprehend. Used to a world in which towns were centers of
administration and trade, inhabited chiefly by Turks and foreign merchants and shopkeepers, peasants were inclined to
identify themselves with the moral essence of national life.
"There are no members of the Serbian nation but peasants,"
pronounced Vuk Karadžic early in the nineteenth century.
Money meant exploitation, shops and commerce implied
degeneration. Some peasants complained that young people
were tempted "to steal food from their homes to procure use-
less, cheap goods at the shop."[43]

But now they found that independence brought no escape
from these evils. They had expelled the Turkish landlords
and officials, only to find that a new governing class had taken
their place, with new means of enrichment and new preten-
sions. "In analyzing the national character," a young British
diplomat commented on *fin de siècle* Serbia, "you have two distinct classes to deal with—the governmental and commercial,
which wears coats, trousers and boots—but not always socks;
and the peasant, which affects jackets, petticoats and san-
dals."[44] The arbitrary and corrupt Ottoman tax farmer had
been superseded by a salaried and modernizing bureaucracy,
eager to replace the old "money anarchy" with a single currency, to send out gendarmes, teachers, surveyors and census
takers to classify, register and chart the land and educate
those who worked it. All this sounded like more interference
and exploitation, not less. The modern Balkan state undoubtedly intruded further into the farmer's life than the Ottoman
state had done; there were more civil servants per capita in
the Balkans than in Germany or Britain. "Better the Turkish
bullet than the Greek pen"—the expression I heard from one
Macedonian peasant in the 1990s—was no doubt uttered by
many of his forebears in the age of Balkan independence.

Yet with only limited success in articulating their griev-
ances in the new parliaments, there was little the peasants
could do about this. Politically their inability to organize cost
them dear. Despite their overwhelming numbers they
remained politically negligible. Other parties co-opted them
through networks of clientilism while the state used the gen-
darme, the schoolteacher and tax collector to keep an eye on
the villages. Independence, therefore, turned out to be the
Balkan peasantry's final victory. Land reforms in the 1920s,
which were a peasant success of sorts, reflected fears among
Balkan politicians that without buying off the peasants, they
might not be able to prevent revolutionary Bolshevism from
subverting society. Yet land reform alone did not guarantee
peasants a living. On the contrary, the outcome by the 1930s
was greater fragmentation of holdings and an even less effi-
cient pattern of land tenure than before. The peasant's political triumph led to his economic ruin. Flight from the land
was inexorable, hindered only by muddy roads and the lack of
prospects elsewhere.

The deeper problem was that peasant values offered no
solution to the demographic and economic dilemmas facing
the new Balkan states. Smallholdings simply did not create
enough wealth, even in good times, to satisfy a newly con-
sumerist society; villages lacked cinemas, phonographs and
the other amusements that dazzled the minds of young people. In the 1930s, Croatian peasant girls "chatted...glibly
about makeup, of patent leather shoes and high heels." They
told a visitor that they preferred finer clothes to better food
on the grounds that "no one can see what I've got inside me,
but all can tell what I've got on." However, economic depression allowed them neither new clothes nor sufficient food.
Between the wars, almost all crops went down in price and
plunged peasants into debt. Interwar economists calculated
that six to eight million of a rural labor force of just under

thirty million had no real work, thanks to what one described as "the vicious circle of population pressure, poverty and lack of industries."[45]

To some extent, the war years allowed country dwellers to gain their revenge on townspeople; for a brief period in the 1940s, to be a producer of food was to be master once more. But when peace returned, the locus of political action and wealth creation reverted to the cities. In 1974 the historian Steven Runciman bemoaned the modern Balkan "megalopolis" that had brought high-rise apartments, traffic jams and atmospheric pollution to the small sleepy capitals he had first visited half a century earlier. But the mountains no longer offered an option for communal life in the way they had done two centuries earlier, and there was no replacing the destroyed forests. Village populations in the Pindos Mountains dropped from thousands in the nineteenth century to a few hundred today. Except through tourism and remittances, there is no way these settlements can continue. The movement of peoples from the hills to the plains has been succeeded by a further movement into the towns. In fifty years, the total share of the working population employed on the land fell from 80 percent to 37 percent in Bulgaria, from 78 percent to 29 percent in Yugoslavia and from 77 percent to 29 percent in Romania. In the Balkans we are dealing no longer with a peasant society, but with its successor.[46]

2

BEFORE THE NATION

The ecclesiastic geography of these degraded regions must of course be only interesting to the mere antiquary, as it can throw no light on its history and little even on its topography.

—JOHN PINKERTON, *MODERN GEOGRAPHY* (1802)

Our church is holy, but our priests are thieves.

—BYRON'S SERVANT

At the beginning of the twentieth century, Greek and Bulgarian patriots wrestled for the allegiance of the Orthodox Christian peasants of Ottoman Macedonia. It turned out to be unexpectedly difficult. "On my arrival in Salonika," wrote one Greek activist, "the idea of Greek peasants and the people on the actual difference between the Greek Orthodox church and Bulgarian schismatics was rather shaky. I realized this because whenever I asked them, what they were—*Romaioi* [i.e., Greeks] or *Voulgaroi* [Bulgarians], they stared at me incomprehendingly. Asking each other what my words meant, crossing themselves, they would answer me naïvely: 'Well, we're Christians—what do you mean, *Romaioi* or *Voulgaroi?*' "[1]

Similarly, the pro-Bulgarian Danil, "a town-made patriot of recent construction" as his English companion described him, "was vexed with the villagers' apathy." Round the Prespa Lake he tried to explain to them that by being forced to listen to the church service in Greek rather than in their own Slavic tongue, they were being exploited by an anti-Bulgarian clergy. "But they bolted raw cabbage and washed it down with mastic and only said it did not matter; many of them spoke Greek. The priest took a suck at the bottle and was of the same opinion. He spoke the local Slavic dialect himself for ordinary purposes, but he had learned all the services in Greek. It was a good service and what did it matter? Danil was very annoyed, and told me that they were very ignorant; really they were all Bulgarians, and ought to have Bulgarian priests, but they did not know. Nor as far as I could see, did they care here."[2]

This indifference to nationalist categories among the Sultan's Christian subjects reflected their sense of belonging to a community defined by religion, where the linguistic differences between Greek and Bulgarian mattered less than their shared belief in Orthodoxy. Such encounters marked the moment when the bearers of the concept of modern ethnic politics infiltrated the countryside and encountered a prenational world. The linguistic, racial and religious diversity of the peoples inhabiting southeastern Europe dates back to the Slav invasions, if not earlier. Politically, however, this counted for little until recently. Neither the Byzantine nor the Ottoman empires were ethnically based polities. For centuries, conversion and acculturation opened up elite careers to men of different backgrounds.

Because the history of the Balkans has mostly been written by descendants of the nationalist patriots described above, the hesitant, ambivalent voices of the peasants they were trying to enlighten rarely make it into the archives. But one can detect, even fairly recently, the persistence of habits of mind that predate the triumph of ethnic politics. "I questioned some boys from a remote mountain village near Ochrida which had neither teacher nor resident priest, and where not a single inhabitant was able to read, in order to discover what amount of traditional knowledge they possessed," wrote H. N. Brailsford in 1905. "I took them up to the ruins of the Bulgarian Tsar's fortress which dominates the lake and the plain from the summit of an abrupt and curiously rounded hill. 'Who built this place?' I asked them. The answer was significant—'The Free Men.' 'And who were they?' 'Our grandfathers.' 'Yes, but were they Serbs or Bulgarians or Greeks or Turks?' 'They weren't Turks, they were Christians.' And this seemed to be about the measure of their knowledge."[3]

The question of whether they were Serbs, Bulgarians or Greeks meant little for Christian peasant boys in the Ottoman system, just as Muslims too attached relatively little importance to their ethnic background. "Hitherto, there has never been any separatist movement, either national or doctrinal, inside Islam," noted a British diplomat in 1912, surprised by the novelty of an Albanian nationalist organization. "All Musulmans, whether Shia or Sunni, Turk, Arab or Kurd, are simply entered on the register as 'Moslems.'" The consciousness of most of the Sultan's subjects was shaped neither by school nor by the army—the two key institutions through which the modern state propagates national identities. The Ottoman state had treated them on the basis of religion, not language. Thus they had not had to encounter such novel forms of classification as were implied by Brailsford's questions, though their grandchildren would take them for granted.[4]

—

One need not look far back into history to see the way in which human migrations have shaped the ethnography of the Balkans. In the twentieth century alone, millions of people have moved, or been moved, from one country to another. In the postwar period, Greek and Yugoslav workers settled in Australia, the United States and Western Europe looking for jobs; in the 1990s, new movements of peoples looking for work or fleeing war formed the latest chapter in a story that has been going on for millennia. Yet, despite this constant ebb and flow, the basic ethnographic composition of the peninsula was established as long ago as the seventh century A.D. Life in the Roman provinces south of the Danube had been disrupted before then by the incursions and raids of Germanic tribes and the Huns. But these invasions, though frequent and often destructive, were brief and usually ended with the raiders moving off elsewhere. The impact of the Slavic tribes was very different: over roughly 200 years, they settled permanently in large numbers to till the land and graze their flocks across the peninsula as far south as the Peloponnese. Their arrival in the Balkans marked the end of the ancient world and had the momentous effect of driving a wedge between the western and eastern halves of the Roman empire that would eventually contribute to the split between Catholicism and Eastern Orthodoxy.[5]

The area's existing inhabitants competed for land and power with the newcomers. In Albania they found refuge in the mountains, preserving their distinct language amid what became a largely Slavic-speaking zone of settlement. The Greeks—who described themselves as Romaioi (inhabitants of the Roman empire) in place of the older "Hellenes" (a term that had come to mean "pagan")—were penned into isolated areas (islands, or into walled towns and depopulated cities) where they preserved the Greco-Roman civic culture of the empire. The Turkic Bulgars, who ruled over Slavic tribes in their khanate around the lower Danube, ended up—much like ruling elites in England, Normandy and Varangian Rus—adopting the language of the peoples they ruled. Right up to the early twentieth century the basic pattern of Slavic-speaking village and Greek-speaking town was preserved in Macedonia.

Initially the linguistic divide between Greeks and Slavs was also a religious one, between Christians and pagans. But in the ninth and tenth centuries, the Slavs were converted to Christianity, as the Greeks had been before them. Cyril and Methodius, the two brothers who undertook this mission, were from Salonika, where they had undoubtedly come into contact with the Slavic language spoken by local peasants: by developing an alphabet and a liturgy in Slavonic, they and their successors brought the Slavs under the sway of the Church at a time when much of eastern and northern Europe remained faithful to older gods. The price to be paid for this success was the sacrifice by the Church of the privileged position of the Greek language in the emergent Orthodox Balkan commonwealth, an attitude that contrasted with the papacy's growing insistence upon Latin: many languages, one Church was the secret of Byzantine Orthodoxy.

The Balkans were too mountainous, too vulnerable and fragmented to make for an easy religious or linguistic homogenization. It was not only the Albanians who sought the protection of the hills. The Vlachs were a shepherding people who preserved their Romance language right up to this century amid Greek- and Slav-speaking majorities; the Sarakatsani were another even smaller nomadic group. Orthodoxy predominated but did not prevail everywhere. The kings of Croatia followed the Latin rite and Catholicism, despite their Slavic background, while in Bosnia a third, Bosnian church spread before disappearing with the arrival of the Turks. A Bulgarian tsar was crowned by the Pope in 1204 while Catholic and later Protestant missionaries devoted their energies—though with little reward outside Albania and the Aegean islands—to proselytizing for the true faith. Small Jewish communities too existed throughout the peninsula.

Greek, as the ruling language during the Byzantine period, and as the language of the Gospels, Christian culture and classical learning through Ottoman times as well, attracted ambitious young Vlach or Slav men—just as Venetian, German and later French would do as well. As late as the 1860s, according to the memoirs of one Ottoman official, Greek was still known to "all Romanians of distinction" and used in preference to Turkish when Ottoman and Romanian notables met. Jewish communities that dated back to classical times acquired Greek as their vernacular tongue. Western Europeans too could turn into Greeks. In 1833, several hundred Bavarian mercenaries accompanied King Otto to Athens: a century later, SS officials, scouring Europe for precious German blood, found their great-grandchildren living on farms in Attica. Most had forgotten German and become Greek-speaking and Orthodox. Of course, hellenization had its limits. North of the old Via Egnatia, Greek made few inroads among the Slavic-speaking villages. In northern Albania and the Danubian provinces, too, its use remained confined to higher church clergy, and in the latter case to the courts of native princes. Even within what would later become Greece, many peasants spoke Albanian until the 1950s. But in general, knowledge of Greek remained the main path to learning, religious authority and political power for as long as the Byzantine empire existed.[6]

The dominion of Greek culture over Balkan Christians was not ended by the collapse of Byzantium between the thirteenth and fifteenth centuries. But it was transformed through the arrival of a new people—Turkish-speaking, Muslim by religion. These Turks defeated the various Christian powers of southeastern Europe—not only the rulers of Byzantium, but also Serb, Genoese, Hungarian, Venetian and other dynasties—and in doing so, unified the region politically and economically in an empire that lasted for five centuries. Before their conquest of the Balkans, the Turks had been active in the region as allies and auxiliaries of the very Christian powers that they later ended up subjugating; after it, they continued to use Christian soldiers, notably in their military campaigns in Anatolia and the Middle East. Christian–Muslim relations were thus based on generations of interaction, and conquest and collaboration more closely resembled patterns evident in the British takeover of India than in the German invasion of Poland.

Even before the fall of Constantinople in 1453, Christians were turning to Islam for many reasons. A fifteenth-century Greek archbishop noted with disgust the voluntary conversion of those who were motivated by "the desire to win silver, become notables and live in luxury." By the early sixteenth century several hundred thousand had probably converted.

Members of the Bosnian and Byzantine nobility, including some of the imperial Paleologue family itself, served the Sultan loyally in high positions both as Christians and increasingly as Muslim converts: when the Ottoman Grand Vizier Mahmud Pasha Angelovic negotiated in 1457 with the Grand Voivode of the Serbian court, Michael Angelovic, he was in fact dealing with his own half brother. And later it was with his cousin, the Byzantine philosopher George Amiroutzis, that Mahmud Pasha negotiated the surrender of the Byzantine province of Trabizond. The Christian Amiroutzis subsequently found refuge at the Ottoman court and was favored by the Sultan; his two sons converted to Islam and became high court officials. The well-connected Mahmud Pasha was himself of Serbian and Byzantine descent; other grand viziers of Mehmed II (the conqueror of Constantinople in 1453) were Greeks or Albanians by birth. Many of these men were children from aristocratic Christian families trained at the imperial court. Others were recruited from low-born peasantry through the child tax levied on Balkan Christian communities.[7]

Until the early seventeenth century, the Ottoman court relied on its slave recruits. "Most of the inhabitants of the land of Rum are of mixed origin," wrote Mustafa Ali in the seventeenth century. "Amongst the more prominent there are few whose genealogies do not go back to a convert to Islam, or whose ethnic origins, either on their mother's or father's side, do not go back to a filthy infidel, despite the fact that they themselves have grown up as upright and outstanding Muslims." The imperial governing elite was admired throughout Europe for its meritocratic character, and observers noted with surprise that the most senior officials often came from families of humble birth. There was no Ottoman hereditary aristocracy—"no Nobilitie of Blood," commented George Sandys in 1610 and "few Turks, generally a term of reproach." Indeed the characterization of the Ottoman system as Turkish was very wide of the mark. As late as the nineteenth century, it was noted that "no Mussulman ever calls himself a Turk; further to call him so is to insult him." (The term was used to refer to Anatolian peasants.) So prominent was the presence of converts at the Porte that for a time Slavic rivaled Turkish as a court language. "The better sort use the Slavonian tongue," observed William Lithgow, "the vulgar speake the Turkish language, which being originally the tartarian speech, they borrow from the Persian their words of state, from the Arabicke, their words of Religion, from the Grecians, their termes of warre, and from the Italian their words and titles of navigation." Lady Mary Wortley Montagu noted that in the capital "they speak Turkish, Greek, Hebrew, Armenian, Arabic, Persian, Russian, Sclavonian, Walachian, German, Dutch, French, English, Italian, Hungarian; and what is worse, there is ten of these Languages spoke in my own family."[8]

If conversion was the prerequisite for individual advancement and a career in government, Islamicization on a mass scale was observable only in a few areas of the Balkans. In Thrace and Macedonia, the first provinces conquered by the Ottomans, villagers from Anatolia were resettled among the Christian inhabitants. But imperial resettlement was not the most important force for Islamicization: in Bosnia, in parts of Bulgaria and later in Cyprus, Albania and Crete, Christian peasants converted in substantial numbers and often en masse. From Bulgaria we read that "all the unbelievers in a village have converted to Islam." "All the inhabitants of a big village of unbelievers have gradually converted to Islam," begins another Ottoman *fatwa*, decreeing the building of a new mosque to serve the community. "More than 40,000 people abandoned Christianity," the bishop of Zagreb wrote in alarm in November 1536. "More and more people are doing so, hoping they will enjoy more peaceful times in remains of their lives."[9]

Mass conversion continued into the late Ottoman period. In Albania, Christians adopted Islam in the eighteenth century. Around the Drina valley, a traveler in the middle of the nineteenth century observed that the mostly Roman Catholic villagers "have been so persecuted of late years that a large number have become Mussulmans."[10]

A compelling argument for conversion was the second-class status of non-Muslims in the Ottoman world. Christians (and Jews) were tolerated as "people of the Book," but they faced discrimination and ill treatment on the grounds of their religion: they were not allowed to ride horses, wear the color green or build churches above a certain height. Their word counted for less than that of a Muslim in Ottoman courts, and they bore heavier taxes, supposedly for not performing military service. Despite these hardships, however, the Balkans retained their predominantly Christian and non-Turkish-speaking character; this stood in sharp contrast to the Ottoman domains in Anatolia, where Turkish and Islam came to prevail over the long centuries from the Seljuk domination onward.[11]

In Ottoman Europe the vast bulk of the population—probably around 80 percent—remained Christian. Even where Islam made inroads into the countryside, it rarely carried the Turkish language along with it: Bosnian Muslims still spoke their native Slavic; the Muslim Ali Pasha of Jannina spoke Albanian and Greek but not Turkish; the Muslim peasants of Crete spoke Greek and enjoyed the Erotokritos, the island's epic poem, as much as the Christians, from whom, after all, most of them were descended. Outside the original heartlands around Edirne, the Turkish language in the Balkans remained an administrative lingua franca confined to urban centers. Cities like Bosna Seraj, Skopje and Sofia were heavily Islamic and Turkish-speaking islands of imperial governance in a mostly Christian sea—much as German-speaking cities functioned in Slavic eastern Europe at the same time.[12]

If the Balkans did not become another Islamic land, one reason was that the sultans had no interest in making this happen. Christians paid higher taxes, and mass conversion would have impoverished the empire. "Very many [Greeks]," reported seventeenth-century travelers, "unable to bear any longer this cruel tyranny, wish to turn Turk; but many are rejected, because (say their lords), in receiving them into the Moslem faith, their tribute would be so much reduced." Less material factors also played a part. On the two occasions (in 1517 and again in 1647) when the Porte seriously considered the forced Islamicization of the Balkan Christians, there was religious opposition to the idea on Koranic grounds. In general, there was no Muslim analogue to the widespread Christian impulse to drive out the infidel and the heretic. On the contrary, Islamic law prescribed the toleration of Christian and Jewish communities of believers. It prohibited Muslims from converting to other religions, but did not insist upon conversion in the other direction. Indeed many a convert was obliged to demonstrate that the desire to embrace the true faith was not prompted by materialistic or ignoble motives.

For Orthodoxy, therefore, Islamic rule was far less damaging than Roman Catholic. Catholic armies had brought destruction to Balkan Christians in the crusades of 1204 and 1444; Venetian rule had been harsh and repressive in Crete and the Peloponnese. After the brief occupation of Chios by the Venetians in 1694, islanders said "they were better off under the Turks." "I'd rather turn Turk than join you Latins who hate and persecute us," an Orthodox monk told a Catholic missionary in 1641. In fact, Orthodox–Catholic relations were often more harmonious inside the empire than outside: in the seventeenth-century Cyclades, for instance,

where there was a small Catholic population, Catholics and
Orthodox islanders often attended each other's services and
built adjacent churches. As late as 1749, the Orthodox patriarchate reprimanded the folk of Sifnos and Mikonos for fail-
ing to recognize any difference between the two rites. But
on the whole few peasants converted from Orthodoxy to
Catholicism, despite the activity of Jesuits and other missionaries across the Balkans. Turkish rule tilted the balance of
power between patriarchate and papacy in favor of the former, not least because the patriarchate—unlike the papacy—
was a servant of the Porte.[13]

In the middle of the eighteenth century, a dispute over
appointments in Antioch suddenly brought home to the Patriarch the dangers of too relaxed an attitude toward Catholic
activity in the empire. It was at this point that—in parallel
with the Porte's own efforts at administrative reform—the
Ecumenical Patriarchate tightened its control over the community of believers, laying the basis for that system of centralized ecclesiastical rule which would come to be known as
the "millet" system. In looser fashion, however, the Orthodox
Church had been brought into the system of Ottoman government much earlier, at least from the time when Sultan
Mehmed II established new guidelines for the administration
of his Christian "flock" (*re'aya*). Christians, like Jews, were recognized as *zimmi* (a protected people) permitted to govern
themselves according to their own customs, provided that they
remained loyal and paid their taxes. The Orthodox patriarchs—preeminent among them the Ecumenical Patriarch of
Constantinople—were guarantors on both counts and over
time came to be regarded as the heads of "the groups of the
infidel." In return, they received the authority to tax the
Orthodox flock for communal purposes, and to administer justice to Christians through Church courts. Their representatives enjoyed official privileges, such as the use of Turkish

soldiers to accompany them when collecting taxes. The Sultan thus handed the Church hierarchy a new role; in addition to the spiritual functions it had carried out in the Byzantine world, it was now gradually drawn into politics and administration as a voice for the empire's Orthodox subjects.[14]

In this way, the Ottoman conquest of the Balkans, far from crushing Christian Orthodoxy, brought it many advantages, as both the patriarchate and its enemies and rivals realized. After the chaos of the final fragmented phase of Byzantine rule, the Church was now able to recover and indeed expand its power both in the Balkans and in Anatolia. Thanks to the Turks, it was largely freed from the threat of Catholicism presented by the Venetians and the Genoese in the eastern Mediterranean. Ottoman power in effect unified the Balkans for the first time in centuries. In the late sixteenth century it was reported from the Ottoman capital that the Christians there "do not want any other domination in preference to the Turks." And when Turkish troops reconquered the Peloponnese from the Venetians in 1715, the Greek peasants welcomed and supported them.[15]

Ottoman rule was bringing Balkan Christians not only religious autonomy but increasing prosperity as well. Right from the start, Christian control of some revenue collecting allowed a few individuals to amass extraordinary wealth. In the fifteenth century, Michael Kantakuzinos, a maker and breaker of patriarchs, was said to consort with pashas and viziers and to be addressed by them in terms of respect. Later, Orthodox merchants took advantage of the collapse of old trading rivals like Venice and the opening up of new markets in central Europe and southern Russia. They built fortunes in trade and created a substantial shipping fleet. Moneyed and Western-educated Greek families in Constantinople— known as Phanariots, after the area of the city where they resided—became go-betweens at the highest levels of the

Ottoman administration, and started to dominate the lay offices of the patriarchate. Greek dragomans (translators) played crucial roles in negotiating the Venetian surrender of Crete in the mid-seventeenth century as well as at the 1698 peace conference of Carlowitz with the Habsburgs, where the remarkable Alexandros Mavrokordatos served alongside the main negotiator, Rami Mehmed Efendi. Mavrokordatos's son was appointed prince in the Danubian autonomous provinces, the first of those Greek princes who, during the eighteenth century, turned Bucharest and Jassy into centers of Hellenic learning and culture, a crucial intersection of Ottoman, Russian, Italian and central European influences. Greek Christians by birth, Ottoman by allegiance and through self-interest, the Phanariots were, in the refined and ambiguous words of one of their most illustrious figures, "as Greek as it is possible to be." Being Greek, for them, meant prestige, wealth and glory in the imperial service of the Sultan. "We conform to the prescription of the Gospel, 'Render unto Caesar's the things which are Caesar's,' " Alexandros Mavrokordatos wrote. "It is not the custom of us Christians to confuse what is temporary and corruptible with what is divine and eternal."[16]

When it came to corruption, the Phanariots had experience. Their rise coincided with growing financial and ethical problems inside the patriarchate. In the century after 1495 there were just nineteen changes of patriarch; the following century there were sixty-one. The Church became notoriously corrupt as its highest offices were bought and sold through huge bribes to Ottoman officials. The money, often borrowed by candidates for office from wealthy Phanariots, could be recouped only through the Church's taxation of Christian peasants. Growing centralization under the Ecumenical Patriarch increased the resources at stake and probably made the problem worse. "A saying common among the

Greek peasants," according to a British traveler, was that "the country labors under three curses, the priests, the *cogia bashis* [local Christian notables] and the Turks, always placing the plagues in this order." In nineteenth-century Bosnia, "The Greek Patriarch takes good care that these eparchies shall be filled by none but Fanariots, and thus it happens that the... Orthodox Christians of Bosnia, who form the majority of the population, are subject to ecclesiastics alien in blood, in language, in sympathies, who oppress them hand in hand with the Turkish officials and set them, often, an even worse example of moral depravity." The reason was clear: "They have to send enormous bribes yearly to the fountainhead." This story of extortion and corruption spelled the end of the old Orthodox ecumenicism, created bitterness between the Church and its flock and, where the peasants were not Greek speakers, provoked a sense of their exploitation by the "Greek" Church that paved the way for Balkan nationalism.[17]

Yet even while corruption was eating into the institutions of the Church, there flourished a world of Balkan Orthodoxy whose horizons stretched from the Mediterranean to the Black Sea, from northern Italy to Russia. The freedom of movement and thought possible for educated and mobile Christians in this Orthodox Balkan commonwealth can be traced in the careers and travels of men such as Iossipos Mosiodax, a distinguished pedagogue and scholar, who was by origin a Vlach from the southern bank of the Danube in present-day Romania. Born in 1725, he was educated and hellenized at schools in Salonika, Smyrna and Mount Athos before studying at Padua and then teaching at the princely academies of Jassy and Bucharest, the centers of Greek learning in the Balkans. Having also traveled to Venice, Vienna and Budapest, he claimed to have seen "all the diasporas of the Greeks." His contemporary, Constantine Dapontes, was born on the island of Skopelos, educated in Constantinople and traveled widely in Ottoman lands. In 1757 Dapontes began an eight-year journey across the Balkans carrying the True Cross of his monastery. He sailed from Athos, and crossed future Bulgarian lands to reach the Danube and Moldavia before returning south to Constantinople—thereby saving the city from a plague, according to his own account, which was raging elsewhere—and returning in triumph to the Holy Mountain in 1765.

Dapontes's peregrinations took place in a world in which his "homeland" was his native island; the term "Greece" had no political or territorial meaning for him. Southeastern Europe was a region marked out not by nation-states but by the symbols of Orthodoxy. Time was measured by the rhythms of the Eastern Church rather than by any secular sense of history. The divine and the supernatural were omnipresent in daily life. Yet Balkan Orthodoxy also had its material rewards: sweet wines from Sámos and Cyprus, pistachios from Aleppo, figs from Smyrna, apples from Moldavia and Wallachian cheeses. When the historian Christopher Dawson asked why it was that the Byzantine empire, unlike the papacy in the West, failed to consolidate its cultural-religious hold in its part of Europe, he missed the point that a Byzantine culture *did* continue to evolve—under the guidance of Orthodoxy and Ottoman imperial rule. It evolved in the stilted writings of the Greek Phanariots of the Sultan's capital, who oscillated between fidelity to the Porte and hopes for a rebirth of the Byzantine empire, but who remained throughout pious supporters of Orthodoxy and hellenism. And it evolved in the hands of a church intellectual like Eugenios Voulgaris—perhaps the most important figure of late-eighteenth-century Orthodoxy—who was educated in his native Corfu (under Venetian rule), in Turkish Jannina and at the University of Padua, before bringing his teachings to Athos, Constantinople and eventually to the

Russia of Catherine the Great, to whom he preached the dangers of a new Catholic advance into eastern Europe.[18]

———

Separate but parallel religious institutions were fundamental to the Ottoman governing machine. The Sultan's subjects were divided into communities on the basis of belief and ruled largely by their own ecclesiastical hierarchy, with rabbis, bishops and *cadis* presiding over courts, supervising civil affairs and assuming responsibility for collecting taxes from their own flock as well as other economic matters. But while religion thus acted to demarcate communities and individuals from one another, and even to divide them, it also constituted a shared outlook upon life's problems and dilemmas. This was especially true under a system of rule that, compared with those current elsewhere in Europe, offered an unparalleled degree of religious tolerance—"there being a Free Liberty of Conscience, for all kinds of Religion, through all his Dominions," in Lithgow's words.[19]

Religious power was a common resource that was feared, respected and consulted by peoples of all faiths. Christians availed themselves of Muslim wisdom, gathering charms or holy ground from mosques or *tekkes* (holy shrines). In the legend of one Christian martyr, we also read how a Muslim woman was cured by the Patriarch: having initially refused to see her, on the grounds that "it is not proper for us to accept those who are foreign to our faith," the Patriarch relented, saying: "Him that cometh to me will I in no wise cast out." And just as Muslims visited Christian priests, so too they visited Jewish rabbis. We read, for example, of a sixteenth-century Istanbul man who vowed in the midst of a dangerous fever that if he recovered he would give up his taste in young boys. Cured, he thought better of it, but hesitated to break his vow. Having been advised by the ulema of Istanbul that he could not wriggle out of an oath once made, he sought the advice of the rabbis of Salonika to see if they could find a loophole. (They suggested he try women.)[20]

People who faced special dangers, such as seafarers, often displayed an ecumenical piety. "When [the Turks'] preparations for a voyage have been made," noted de Busbecq, "they come to the Greeks and ask whether the waters have been blessed; and if they say that they have not been blessed, they put off their sailing, but if they are told that the ceremony has been performed, they embark and set sail." Sailors of all faiths—especially pirates and corsairs—revered icons of the Virgin Mary. Caught in a storm, a Frenchman was urged by a Turkish sailor to pray for the Virgin's help, since he had heard, while a captive in Vienna, that her intercession was helpful. In this world one needed help from whatever quarter: impiety was far more grievous than belonging to a different faith. An English slave on a Turkish warship recounted how

> at their first coming on board, they had been asked of what religion they were, and upon declaring themselves Catholic Christians, some mild endeavors had been used to persuade them to renounce their faith, and to become Mohametans; but upon their steady denial, they were told that, since they refused to embrace the true faith, they must as the next best chance for salvation, serve God in their own way; and immediately a small cabin was alloted them, which they were desired to fit up as a chapel, and in which they were compelled to pray daily and regularly.[21]

Plagues, droughts, floods, earthquakes, pirates, wars and fires—all the afflictions and hazards of ordinary life in the Ottoman Balkans—compelled a respect for heavenly powers and for wisdom and knowledge of the divine among humans that ran across religious boundaries. Specific saints, for instance, were known for their protection of particular cities; their ability to ward off danger was recognized by Christians and Muslims alike. "Both the Christians and the Turks were

indeed of religion itself) held by the onlookers—the Western visitors, the scholars, the senior clerics on the lookout for doctrinal error, the professional heretic hunters—than it did on the ordinary peoples of the Balkans and their priests. To a French scholar of the early twentieth century, the peasants did not seem "very enlightened." But such comments assumed that religion too should be a matter of "enlightenment," premised upon sharply elucidated doctrine—a view that made more sense among literate, urban elites than for illiterate Orthodox country folk, for whom practice mattered far more than dogma. It assumed as well that religion was a matter of the private, reflective conscience, a question of theology rather than of collective beliefs and practices; it demarcated religion sharply from the world of science and technical knowledge on the one hand, and from that of magic and the supernatural on the other. If Orthodox priests were on the whole less literate and educated in theological niceties than their Catholic equivalents, it was because in the Balkans pietism and moral guidance mattered less than ritual and proper observance.[26]

Another, more sympathetic approach to popular religion sees in it the desire to avoid life's risks, to explain and if possible forestall its pitfalls and tragedies. It is, in other words, a form of peasant rationality: garlic keeps away the evil eye; holy soil or relics, if gathered in the right way, and collected while the priest or *hodja* uttered the name of a family member, could be kept for use in an emergency if that person fell ill or had an accident. At the extreme, this kind of interpretation reduces religion to a form of insurance. But it has the merit of recognizing what the peasantry themselves were free to admit, that differences of doctrine were not usually very important to them. In poorly churched rural areas, this even led to considerable slippage between what outsiders (including the Ottoman state) regarded as distinct religions. "The

Mahometans here are not real Mahometans," observed a Turkish telegraph operator in early-twentieth-century Albania, "and the Christians are not real Christians." Lady Mary Wortley Montagu noted: "The people who live among Christians and Muslims and are not versed in controversy, declare themselves absolutely incapable of judging which is the better religion: but to be certain of not rejecting the truth, with very great prudence they observe both and go to mosque on Friday and church on Sunday." Asked what religion they were, the cautious peasants of western Macedonia would cross themselves and say, "We are Muslims, but of the Virgin Mary." Centuries earlier, struck by the presence of Turks at Greek rites on the island of Lemnos, Busbecq had heard similar sentiments: "If you ask them why they do this, they reply that many customs have survived from antiquity the utility of which has been proved by long experience; the ancients, they say, knew and could see more than we can, and custom which they approved ought not to be wantonly disturbed."[27]

In this shared world, devotional practice cut across theological divides not only in the realm of the supernatural but also in the daily, mundane life of the Ottoman world. Islamic courts and Turkish administration, for instance, were available for non-Muslims as well as for Muslims. The former could use them as a court of appeal, but also on occasions as a means of bypassing their own religious authorities or customary courts. Thus Muslim officials helped Christians and Jews settle tax, commercial and land affairs in accordance with Islamic law. Local Ottoman governors in the sixteenth and seventeenth centuries sometimes even intervened to settle local disputes over episcopal appointments within their Christian communities. Muslims, Christians and Jews were members of the guilds that borrowed from the Byzantine practice of putting themselves under the protection of a protecting saint, sheik or holy man. Orthodox men and women sometimes used the *sharia* courts even when no Muslims were involved. "I sold my son a cow," ran the complaint of one Christian peasant from Cyprus before an Islamic judge. "I want the money. He is stalling. I want it in accordance with the *sharia*."[28]

The most intimate areas of personal life were shaped by this coexistence of religions. Christian church attitudes toward marriage, for instance, faced unexpected competition. Under Islam, both polygamy and forms of temporary marriage contracts were available, divorce was easier to obtain (especially for women), and sex was neither confined to marriage nor validated solely by procreation. There was little question which religion possessed the more intrinsically attractive possibilities. The church hierarchy appears to have held the line on polygamy (which was, in any event, not common among Balkan Muslims); but temporary marriages were a different matter. The practice of contracting a liaison with a woman for a specified sum over a limited period, noted as early as 1600 by William Biddulph, had a natural appeal to Christians as well as Muslims. Eventually the church was forced to acquiesce in this practice, which became fairly widespread during the eighteenth century. In some areas, it turned into a means of earning a dowry, a kind of legitimized prostitution: "If a stranger should wish to enjoy anyone of the young unmarried women," noted a bemused Lord Charlemont in the Cyclades,

he addresses himself immediately to her parents, and demands the girl in marriage. The bargain is presently struck, and the couple are brought before a magistrate, where they swear mutual fidelity during the man's residence on the island, the bridegroom engaging to pay at his departure a great sum of money, as well as a present advance.... This money is set apart in the girl's portion, and with this, upon the departure of her consort, she soon procures herself a real husband among her countrymen, who esteem her not a whit the less for this previous connection, deeming her a widow to all intents and purposes.

This was the adaptation of Islamic practice by Christian islanders for their own convenience, ratified by Turkish officials and tolerated by village priests.[29]

Aside from this specific device, marriages took place between Muslim men and Christian women in the Balkans as long as the Ottoman empire survived. The result was that many Muslims had Christian mothers, and hence a private familiarity with, and sometimes attachment to, the maternal religion. The Serbian despot George Brankovic married his daughter, Mara, to the Sultan Murad II in 1435, probably in a vain attempt to gain the latter's favor. Ali Pasha of Jannina had a Greek Christian wife, for whom he was reputed to have built a chapel. Later still, the Albanian-born Ottoman official Ismail Kemal Bey would marry a Greek woman, abducting her (with her consent) in order to overcome the objections of her stepmother. And below the level of the elite, there were numerous other instances of Christian–Muslim relationships.[30]

Conversion offered Christian women trapped in unhappy marriages particular advantages. By converting to Islam, they automatically obtained an annulment of their marriage, unless their Christian spouse converted too. There was a special formula for this. "Cako was honored with Islam in the presence of Muslims," a *cadi* court heard, "and she took the name Fatma. Her husband was offered a chance to go to Islam but he declined." In a similar case, a woman named Fatma bint Abdullah registered her conversion to Islam, and it was noted that "my husband Yanno bin Manolya was invited to submit to Islam but he did not become a Muslim. He acknowledges that he has no claim against Fatma." It is striking that Muslim marriages too were affected by the merest suggestion of apostasy. As we read in an eighteenth-century Islamic legal compendium:

> QUESTION: Zeyd and his wife Hind go to church and approve certain actions of the infidels, which entail unbelief. Must Zeyd and Hind undergo a renewal of Faith and a renewal of marriage?
>
> ANSWER: Yes.[31]

In an article written in 1993, Samuel Huntington, an American political scientist, discerned in the war in Bosnia a "clash of civilizations" and situated the Balkans on one of the global fault lines of this clash. Whatever the merits of this as a vision of the future, it must now be evident that it cannot serve as a model of the region's past. The Ottoman state and its religious leaders marked out clear distinctions among Islam, Orthodoxy and Catholicism; but in daily life these distinctions were less pronounced. In this border zone in the Eurasian balance of power, many potential frictions, whether indigenous or brought in by outsiders, were blunted or defused by shared local practices.

Customs evolved to offer security and insurance across the religious divides. In the ceremony of blood brotherhood, young men of different families, and even different religions, swore loyalty to each other. From Livno—where Venetian, Habsburg and Ottoman power collided—we have a Turkish account of a battle in the mid-seventeenth century that ended with the capture of numerous Christian prisoners. When, as was customary, the victorious pasha ordered the execution of his share of the captives, one of his own soldiers pleaded for the life of one of the prisoners to be spared. Asked for an explanation, the soldier replied: "During the battle, I gave this infidel my religion and I took his. We have claimed each other as brothers. If you kill him he will go to paradise with my religion and it will be too bad for poor me."

When the bewildered pasha turned to his other troops, they clarified the custom for him:

> When one of our *yunaks* [auxiliary soldiers] on these frontiers falls captive to the infidels, while eating and drinking with them, one infidel may pledge to save him from captivity, and the Muslim, too, promises to rescue him from the Turks if he falls captive to us. They make a pact, saying: "Your religion is mine and my religion is yours." They lick each other's blood and the infidel and the Muslim become "brothers in religion." ... True, nothing of this sort is found in the books of the Muslims, or of the infidels. Nevertheless, this heresy is quite common in these frontier regions.

The disgusted pasha set both men free.[32]

The blurring of the divide among the three great monotheistic faiths was a feature of one of the fastest-growing religious movements of the seventeenth- and eighteenth-century Balkans—the strain of Islamic mysticism known as Bektashism. Bektashi doctrine, counterposed to the formal hierarchies of Sunni Islam, asserted that "a saint belongs to the whole world." According to a late-nineteenth-century pamphlet, "The Bektashi believe in the Great Lord and in the true saints Mohammed Ali, Kadije, Fatima, and Hasan and Husain.... They also believe in all the saints, both ancient and modern, because they believe in Good and worship it. And as they believe in these and love them, so also do they in Moses and Miriam and Jesus and their servants." The Bektashi adapted Christian saints' shrines and renamed them after their own; other sites, which genuinely were founded by the Bektashi, were visited by Christians as sanctuaries of their saints. In such a setting, religious boundaries dissolved easily. "I thought you were all Moslems here," a British traveler asked the priests at one Bektashi *tekke*. "So we are," they told her, "but of course we keep Saint George's Day." Linked for centuries to the slave converts at the Ottoman court, Bektashism spread throughout southeastern Europe with the empire and became popular in much of southern Albania, where it remains entrenched even after the fall of communism.[33]

Albania was perhaps a special case from the point of view of religion. "We Albanians have quite peculiar ideas," one notable told Edith Durham. "We will profess any form of religion which leaves us free to carry a gun. Therefore the majority of us are Moslems." "The light way religion hangs on an Albanian" was familiar to many in the nineteenth century, but leaving the "world of ignorance" of "the infidel religion" for "the true faith" was for many in the Ottoman world a less momentous or sudden step than it has come to seem to us, for whom conversion summons up images of apostasy, existential angst and personal and national betrayal. Movement into a new faith was often an accretion of new beliefs to older ones rather than an act of renunciation and immersion. Indeed, converts frequently preserved older religious practices and habits, though they often had to keep these secret, to avert the suspicion that their attachment to Islam was not entirely sincere: they painted red eggs at Easter, while Muslim converts from Judaism—the mysterious Donmeh—were said to preserve their old religious practices in the privacy of their homes.[34]

The uses of secrecy also lay behind the custom of double naming, in which a Suleiman turns out also to be known as Constantine, Hussein as Giorgi. A double name allowed one to dodge between inconvenient official categories, also serving to keep a man's real name hidden: Franciscan priests in Albania threw up their hands in horror when their charges persisted in calling themselves not by the baptismal Christian name, but by an assumed Muslim one, but the young men who did this could not be brought to abandon the practice.

What better way, they urged in self-defense, to prevent a witch laying a curse on one than concealing one's real name? Whether against sorcery, or tax farmers or in some cases against the investigators of the Venetian Inquisition, multiple names were a weapon of the weak against the strong, of the private individual against the greater powers of the divine and the secular world. Revelation of one's real name thus marked a decisive moment of individual assertion against power. The life of Saint Elias preserves the fateful conversation that preceded his martyrdom. Having been led to embrace Islam, as we are told, by his desire to escape heavy taxation, the saint is asked: "Are you not Moustafa Ardouris?" "Yes, it is I," he replied. "But I am not Moustafa, rather I am Elias, the Orthodox Christian."[35]

———

The boundaries among religions were not completely permeable, however, and coexistence did not mean toleration. "The Armenian (and the Greek) were dogs and pigs... to be spat upon," notes a British ethnographer in the late nineteenth century. Even before then, members of the ruling religion were often contemptuous in daily speech of the "infidel dogs." Travelers were impressed by the variety of insults in general use:

> Pera is called the *hog's quarter,* perhaps because contrary to the custom of the Turks, the Franks inhabiting it eat hog's flesh; and the Turkish soldiers (who are appointed to attend on foreign ambassadors) are termed *swine herds.* They call the Italians, *people of a thousand colors,* that is to say, *cheats;* the English, *linendrapers;* the French *knaves;* the Germans *roistering swearers;* the Spaniards, *idlers;* the Russians *cursed ones,* the Poles *chattering infidels,* the Venetians *fishermen,* the Wallachians *rats,* the Moldavians *sheep without horns* or *stupid boors,* the Greeks *hares,* the Armenians *dirt eaters,* the Jews *dogs,* the Arabians *silly fellows,* the Persians *red-heads* or *heretics,* the Tartars *carrion-eaters.*

"Abdi called me infidel, son of an infidel," complained Mustafa bin Mehmed in a seventeenth-century Ottoman court, outraged at suffering the kind of abuse routinely inflicted upon the "false believers." "Mehmed [Bey] called me a Jew," asserted another.[36]

Christians could not so easily complain. Their second-class status was brought home in the widespread conversion of many of their churches into mosques. They rarely obtained permission to build new churches, especially in areas inhabited also by Muslims, and they could not ring church bells in such areas but had to call the faithful by beating wooden boards with clappers. ("In Servia [sic]," a French traveler from the Levant noted in 1836, "the Christian religion is entirely unrestricted. We were agreeably surprised by the sounds of bells which we had not heard for so long.") But even this was sometimes regarded as a provocative demonstration of "infidelity" and banned.[37]

In the countryside, the differences between Muslim and Christian were not hidden, and the two communities lived side by side. Nor were their daily interactions always characterized by tension or conflict. A Bulgarian memoir of life in the 1870s recollected:

Turks and Bulgarians got on well together. The women of a village quarter bordering on Turkish houses mixed with the Turkish women in a neighborly way, while the children played with the little Turks as with their own playmates. The Turkish women and children spoke Bulgarian quite well and the Bulgarians, like their children, managed to get by in Turkish, the result being a sort of mixed patois. Those Turks who worked at Bulgarian houses were accepted as close friends.... We were used to the Turks. We Bulgarians lived our own life, to be sure, we had our own dress, our own customs and stuck to our own faith, while they lived another way, had other customs and other costume, their faith was different too. But all this we took as being in the order of things.[38]

In the cities, where the Muslim presence was stronger, the dynamics of interaction were often rather different, marked by concentrations of rumor, of fanaticism and of violence against non-Muslims. Constantinople was a dangerous place for non-Muslims until the early nineteenth century; at Ramadan they kept off the streets if they were prudent. In the seventeenth and eighteenth centuries, the janissaries often attacked Christians and Jews with impunity. After the elimination of the janissary corps, this threat declined and modernization brought the emergence of a new, shared bourgeois culture, which again ran across religious boundaries. For the first time, patterns of settlement in the larger urban areas were based on class rather than religion. The houses of prosperous Christians, which before the liberalizing Tanzimat reforms usually had a deliberately unprepossessing exterior so as not to attract attention, became more grand and ostentatious in the latter decades of the nineteenth century. Muslims, Christians and Jews mingled in the labor unions, guilds and bourgeois clubs of Salonika. Class distinctions may not have effaced religious categories, but they created other bonds of solidarity and interest.

Or might have done had the empire appeared more stable. The condition of intercommunal relations was a matter of time as well as space. The rise of Catholic Austria and Orthodox Russia brought new tensions to the empire's religions. Relations between the Orthodox and Catholic Church worsened markedly from the middle of the eighteenth century; earlier they had been surprisingly cordial and cooperative. And in the nineteenth century, of course, the emergence of Greek and Serbian nationalist movements challenged Ottoman attitudes toward Orthodoxy. Hence the moment of apparent constitutional liberalism in the empire was also that of growing Muslim unease at Christian hostility. Hundreds of thousands of embittered Tartar and Circassian refugees, fleeing

Russia's advance to the Black Sea, arrived in Ottoman lands and settled in the Danubian provinces and Bulgaria.

In particular, the reign of Abdul Hamid II from 1876 saw the Ottoman reaction against Western meddling in the empire's affairs. The 1876 constitution defined Islam as the "religion of state," and increasingly popular and official anger against Great Power intervention took the form of mob violence, which exploded in massacres of Armenians in 1895 and Greek Christians on Crete the following year. As a recent historian has remarked, the Ottomans interpreted the Western demand for "freedom of religion" as freedom to defend their religion from the insult of Christian disrespect. The decline of Ottoman power intensified the sense of defensiveness among Muslims in this newly assertive Christian world. Modernity was thus sharpening the religious boundaries between communities in the last phase of imperial rule and giving them a new political edge.[39]

The older attitudes that were disappearing are evoked in the story of the martyrdom of a seventeenth-century bishop of Larissa. "Being of evil mind and evil conduct," we are told, he "was beguiled by the words and promises of certain Europeans and with the cooperation of the devil, and having gathered a sufficient multitude, he declared war upon the Turks, who reigned then.... After a short space of time he was captured and paid the just price of his deeds, being miserably put to death by the Turks, with the permission of God, he having done that which was unworthy of his calling."[40]

This story describes a world of rebellious Christian bishops and merciless Turks. But the Christian cleric is not a hero in the eyes of the (Christian) narrator, as he would be to later nationalist historians; he is a man led astray by the devil. The Turks may be cruel, but they kill the bishop in accordance with God's will. This story does not, then, describe a society free of conflict or religious antagonism. It depicts a violent and restless world, but also a world where Christians owe loyalty to a Muslim state, above all where human action is still understood in religious, not national terms.

—

The Christian peasantry may have been influenced heavily in their beliefs, tastes and practices by Muslim culture, but at the same time they carefully preserved folk songs and ancestral legends about the rebirth of a Christian empire. Predictions, laments and prophecies had circulated among them ever since the fall of Constantinople that fateful Tuesday in 1453. Serb Orthodox bishops and Maniote chieftains were constantly conspiring with Venetian and Austrian diplomats to revolt against the Turks. In 1657 a patriarch was hanged for rashly predicting the end of Islam and the revival of Christian domination. Russia's emergence as the first great European Orthodox power prompted prophecies about a race of blond warriors coming from the north to drive the Muslims from Constantinople, the latest in a long line of such forecasts of Christian reconquest and Ottoman defeat. In 1766, a man claiming to be Tsar Peter III, Catherine the Great's unfortunate (and dead) husband, appeared in Montenegro and led a coalition of clans against the Turks. The impostor's activities provoked Catherine herself to send envoys there to proclaim her support for an uprising that would extend to "Constantinople itself, capital of the ancient Greek empire." The Montenegrins were not interested, of course, in recapturing Constantinople, but Catherine certainly was, and delegated her favorite, Count Aleksey Orlov, to incite an Orthodox revolt against the Porte. Local Greek organizers of the 1770 uprising helped out, even if they regarded Orlov as a man whose "imagination was inflamed from reading ancient history and mythological tales."[41]

Orlov proclaimed Russia's desire for "raising and liberating...the whole Greek nation." But although the local Christian peasants of the Peloponnese and Crete responded with enthusiasm, the revolt was crushed without difficulty by Ottoman forces. Forty thousand people were killed, enslaved or fled the region in 1770. Was this a proto-nationalist revolt? Perhaps. After all, in 1774 the Archimandrite Varlaam wrote to Catherine the Great that her successes "will undoubtedly serve to accelerate the much desired moment of our complete liberation." But in 1779, Greek chieftains cooperated with an Ottoman army in the Peloponnese, and negotiated with the illustrious Greek Phanariot Nicholas Mavroyeni, in order to put down the Albanian irregulars who had been plundering the region. Inside the Ottoman empire there were many Christians, especially in the elite, who saw Russia's failure as a warning, especially since it falsified widely believed predictions of the Sultan's defeat. "If God, constrained by our sins—may He forgive me for daring to say so—prevented that which was affirmed by the oracles from happening at the appointed time," wrote Constantine Dapontes,

> if, I say, He saw fit that the utterances of so many astronomers, scholars and saints should prove vain in preference to giving the Empire to men unworthy not only of this Empire but of life itself, how is it possible that the resurrection of the Romaic Empire should happen ... ? This being so, neither the Greeks nor the Russians will reign in the City unto the end of the world. May merciful God take pity on us, and grant us the Heavenly Kingdom, and never mind about the earthly one.[42]

Yet curiously, Dapontes himself, for all his resignation, was one of those Orthodox intellectuals who, by spreading the ideas of the European Enlightenment into the Balkans, provided a new vocabulary for imagining a post-Ottoman world. Initially their contribution was not explicitly political at all: trained in the new humanistic learning of central Europe, and keen to synthesize this with Orthodoxy, they preached the virtues of scientific knowledge, classical learning and philosophy and attacked the backwardness and barbarism of their own culture. With the spread of print culture, their writings multiplied: seven times as many books were printed annually in Greek by Greeks at the end of the eighteenth century as at its start.[43] Almost all such intellectuals emerged out of the bosom of the church and came to learning through the priesthood. Yet though they did not realize it, their devotion to scientific rationalism on the one hand, and to a secular rather than a biblical sense of history on the other, undermined the traditional bases of religious authority.

It is this small literate elite who, while the vast majority of Ottoman Christians continued to inhabit the mental world described earlier, began to elaborate a new language of nations and ethnicities. The historian Paschalis Kitromilides has described their goal as aiming to integrate "the forgotten nations of the European periphery into the common historical destiny of the Continent." Replacing the old Orthodox conception of Christian time with a new secular understanding of time as national history, the intellectuals of the Balkan Enlightenment paved the way for modern nationalism. At the beginning of the eighteenth century, the Phanariot Alexander Mavrokordatos had divided history into six periods—from the Creation to the Second Coming—that would be followed by a seventh period of "endless repose in the eternal mansions." It was this biblical conception of time—in which historical epochs were believed to correspond to the days of the week—that was eroded by the new emphasis on the unfolding of civilizations and cultures: ancient Greece (in the eighteenth century) and Byzantium (in the nineteenth) became aspects of the past first to be rediscovered, and then to be renewed through political mobilization. History acquired direction.

For much of the eighteenth century, the intellectuals' dreams of political emancipation rested—as Voltaire's did—

upon an enlightened despot coming to their rescue, a Platonic philosopher-king, a modernizer, in the mold perhaps of Catherine the Great or Holy Roman Emperor Joseph II. The Russians remained a source of potential aid, notably during the 1806–1812 Russo-Turkish War, which brought Russian troops south of the Danube and made it look as if "Grandfather Ivan" would liberate Balkan lands. However, it was the French Revolution which first suggested that emancipation might come through the action of the masses themselves. The toppling of the French monarchy, the rise of Bonaparte and, above all, his invasion of Ottoman Egypt in 1798, radicalized the political thought of Balkan Christian intellectuals.[44]

Among the new breed of firebrands was a former secretary of the Phanariots, Rhigas Velestinlis, who published Greek-language literature from Vienna calling for the overthrow of the Ottoman dynasty and the formation of a new republic, based on the rights of man. Rhigas's *New Political Constitution of the Inhabitants of Rumeli, Asia Minor, the Archipelago and the Danubian Principalities* (1797) was the blueprint for a new "Hellenic Republic": the people would be sovereign, irrespective of language or religion. Modern eyes, attuned to future ethnic divisions, are struck by Rhigas's assumption that the new state should use Greek as its official language. What struck contemporaries even more, though, was the absence of any reference to the church. For Rhigas, the Ottoman dynasty and Orthodox Church were both to be swept aside in favor of an as yet ill-defined "Nation."[45]

Such radicalism frightened many, Muslim and Christian alike, by its godlessness and egalitarianism. Ottoman officials denounced "the conflagration of sedition and wickedness that broke out a few years ago in France, scattering sparks and shooting flames of mischief and tumult in all directions." But in Austria the Habsburg authorities were no happier, and arrested Rhigas and handed him over to the Ottomans, who had him killed in 1798. The Orthodox Church was also worried. The concept of political liberty, according to many bishops, was inspired by the devil, tempting the faithful away from their duty of allegiance to the Sultan. The patriarchal "Paternal Exhortation," published in the year of Rhigas's death, inveighed against "the much vaunted system of liberty which...is a trap of the devil and a destructive poison" and reminded Christians how God "raised out of nothing this powerful empire of the Ottomans, in the place of the Roman [Byzantine] Empire which had begun in a certain way to deviate from the Orthodox faith, and he raised up the empire of the Ottomans higher than any other kingdom so as to show without any doubt that it came about by divine will." An anti-intellectual Greek satire that circulated in Constantinople at about the same time mocked the Francophiles: "Romantic youths, enlightened notables" who "say, 'I am enlightened, and I speak French, I myself will wear clothes in the European style.'" There was, in other words, both elite and popular resistance to the political ramifications of the new learning.[46]

Slowly, too, the old assumption that Greek—like Latin in the West—was the route to learning was being challenged as ideas of romantic nationalism, emphasizing the cultural value of peasant languages, spread into the Balkans. In the early nineteenth century, Bulgarian, Serbian and Romanian intellectuals—often educated in Greek schools—began to define themselves in terms of cultural communities for the first time. They chafed under what they saw as Greek domination, doubting openly whether Greek was their language, or "Hellas" their fatherland. "There are those," wrote Paisii Khilandarski in his *Slavonian Bulgarian History*, "who do not care to know about their own Bulgarian nation and turn to foreign ways and foreign tongues; they do not care for their own Bulgarian language but try to read and speak Greek and are ashamed to call themselves Bulgarians."[47]

But at the time few in Khilandarski's target audience would have been able to read Bulgarian. The new ideas of political and cultural affiliation took time to trickle from the intellectuals, books and cities down into the small market towns and the homes of the unlettered mass of country folk, from the diasporas of Vienna, Trieste, Jassy and Odessa to the heartlands of the Sultan's domains. Most people remained illiterate, ignorant of books and the new doctrines they contained, inhabitants of a much more circumscribed rural world. As late as 1810, for instance, there were only two elementary schools in the Pasalik of Belgrade (the core of future Serbia), and in both the language of instruction was Greek; in Montenegro the first elementary school opened in 1834; Romanianism was associated with the desires of the nobility to be rid of their Greek princes, and left the peasantry cold; as for Bulgarian nationalism, it had to await the opening of a few purely Bulgarian schools in the middle of the century.[48]

As nationalism began to eat away at its old constituencies, the patriarchate tried to respond. Its traditional position, both accepting the distinctiveness of different Christian groups and insisting upon their common religious allegiance, was expressed thus by Archbishop Ignatius:

> The Hellenes, the Bulgarians, the Vlachs, the Serbs and the Albanians form today nations, each with its own language. All these people, however, as well as those inhabiting the east, unified by their faith and by the Church, form one body and one nation under the name of Greeks, or Romans [*Romaioi*]. Thus the Ottoman government, when addressing its Christian Orthodox subjects calls them generally Romans, and the Patriarch it always calls Patriarch of the Romans.[49]

But the position of the "Patriarch of the Romans" was being undermined on several sides. Greek intellectuals wrote him off as a quisling "who is either a fool or has been transformed from a shepherd into a wolf." Slav intellectuals increasingly regarded him as a Greek. The Turks mistrusted him as a disloyal servant of the Porte, and in 1821 Patriarch Grigorios V, despite having issued a letter excommunicating the Greek revolutionaries, was executed.[50]

The emergence of Balkan nation-states after 1830 whittled away patriarchal power further. Self-governing peoples in southeastern Europe could not tolerate (any more than the Russians had done in the seventeenth century) the supreme religious direction of their citizens remaining in the hands of an Ottoman government official. "The eastern church is everywhere joined to the state, never being separated from it, never divided from the sovereigns since Byzantine times, and always subordinated to them," wrote one partisan of the new Church of Greece, which was formed in Athens in 1833—without the approval of the Patriarch in Constantinople. Others followed suit: the Bulgarians (even before they had gained an independent state) won a church of their own in 1870—the so-called exarchate—after a long quarrel with the Patriarch over the need for priests who could conduct services in Slavonic. The following year, an autocephalous Romanian church was established. A draft law setting up a Turkish Orthodox church was even submitted to the National Assembly in Ankara in 1921—the logical culmination of the same process. A separate Albanian Orthodox church followed in 1929. Only the Serbs went the canonical route and obtained Patriarchal authorization in 1879 to set up a church of their own. Each of these acts resulted in rupture with the Constantinople patriarchate, which saw its flock gradually dwindling; in each case, the patriarchate was eventually obliged to bow to new political realities. In exactly a century, the Patriarch's flock shrank dramatically, from the entire Orthodox population of the Balkans and Anatolia to a few tens of thousands of believers, mostly in Constantinople itself. The most powerful, wealthiest and successful Christian institution of the Ottoman empire was virtually destroyed by the rise of Christian nation-states.[51]

However, the Balkan Enlightenment did not have it all its own way either. Its liberal and increasingly nationalist intellectuals might have attacked the Church as part of their argument for the existence of national communities, but it was the peasants whose uprisings actually created the new nation-states, and they remained firmly attached to their Church. Catholic missionaries had failed to make substantial inroads into Balkan peasant Orthodoxy; American Protestant missionaries in the 1820s printed more than a million tracts and educated scores of young boys at a cost of a quarter of a million dollars—all for three conversions. It is scarcely surprising that the atheism of many eighteenth-century Balkan intellectuals fell on stony ground. Christian Orthodoxy (and religion in general) remained a major political factor in the Balkans after the collapse of the Ottoman empire. But its character changed. Religion became a marker of national identity in ways not known in the past, and therefore more sharply marked off from neighboring religions. It turned into what the novelist George Theotokas called "a national religion" which left no space for the kind of antichurch secularism that emerged in Western Europe and Italy in the struggle against Catholicism. Today, while the Catholic papacy remains a major political force in the world, the Patriarch of Constantinople barely clings to life, with jurisdiction over the few remaining Orthodox inhabitants of Turkey. In southeastern Europe the modern nation-state—an entity no more than two centuries old—has entirely defeated the old Orthodox values.[52]

3

EASTERN QUESTIONS

The world's great age begins anew
The golden years return…
Heaven smiles, and faiths and empires gleam
Like wrecks of a dissolving dream.

—PERCY BYSSHE SHELLEY[1]

If we enquire into the causes of the internal decline of the Turkish Empire, and regard them under their most general manifestation, we must affirm that it is owing to the fact that the empire is opposed to another section of the world immeasurably superior to itself in power. That other section could crush it to atoms in a moment; and while suffering it to exist for reasons of its own, yet by a secret necessity, it exerts upon it an indirect and invisible influence.

—LEOPOLD VON RANKE[2]

Over the long nineteenth century, which stretched from the French Revolution to the final collapse of the Ottoman Empire in 1923, the political map of the modern Balkans emerged. Independent states formed according to the principle of nationality replaced the five-hundred-year-old empire of the self-styled successor of the Romans, "God's slave and sultan of this world," the Ottoman Padishah. The triumph of nationalism was partly due to the efforts of the Balkan peoples themselves, who had helped shake off Ottoman rule through their uprisings and resistance. But their efforts alone were fruitless until Europe's Great Powers intervened in their favor. The First World War was the culmination of this entangling of Balkan liberation struggles with the European state system.

Foreign schemes for ending Turkish dominion in the Balkans went back to the fifteenth century, but became plausible only once Christian states began to put the Porte on the defensive. After 1699, Austria conquered Hungary-Croatia. Russia reached the Black Sea, and in 1774, having destroyed the Turkish navy in a protracted war, gained treaty rights to intervene in Ottoman affairs to ensure orderly government in the Danubian Principalities, and also to act as protector of the Porte's Christian subjects. It was Poland, not Turkey, that was ultimately the victim of these two predatory powers (together with Prussia) at the end of the eighteenth century. (One unintended consequence was that nation-states would emerge in southeastern Europe several generations earlier than elsewhere in eastern Europe.) The Polish partitions, however, did not sate the appetite of these monarchs.[3]

In a plan drawn up by Joseph II and Catherine the Great to divide the Balkans, Austria was to take over Bosnia and Hercegovina, part of Serbia, Dalmatia and Montenegro, while Russia would control the rest. Catherine's grandson— the deliberately named Constantine—would eventually sit on the throne of a reconstituted Byzantine empire in Istanbul. In 1787, the Austrian and Russian monarchs traveled together through Russia's newly won Black Sea territories, passing under a triumphal arch with the inscription "The Way to Byzantium." But Catherine's "Greek Project" never happened, for too many of the other Great Powers were interested in preventing it, and she had to rest content with annexing the Crimea.[4]

Far from supporting Balkan independence movements, these enlightened despots envisaged substituting Christian imperial rule for Muslim—the replacement of the Sultan by autocratic dynasties ruling over ever vaster polyglot realms of their own. The French Revolution, however, altered many of their assumptions. "According to my judgment," wrote the Greek fighter Théodoros Kolokotrónis in his memoirs, "the French Revolution and the doings of Napoleon opened the eyes of the world. The nations knew nothing before, and the people thought that kings were gods upon the earth and that they were bound to say that whatever they did was well done. Through this present change it is more difficult to rule the people." Indeed, while the Russians continued to see themselves as supporters of Orthodoxy against the Turks, the Habsburgs became increasingly conservative, and from Metternich on, disliked the Slav liberation struggles on their doorstep. France and Britain wavered between supporting oppressed Christians against Muslim despotism and preserving the Ottomans against Russia. Balkan aspirations for self-rule were thus constrained by the competing and clashing interests of the Great Powers. "The more one thinks about the immense question of the fall of the Turkish Empire," wrote Karl Nesselrode, the Russian foreign minister in 1829, "the more one plunges into a labyrinth of difficulty and complications." The international management of this unpredictable process of Ottoman decline and national insurgence became known as the Eastern Question.[5]

Despite the empire's decay, Balkan Christians were too weak to win freedom without foreign support. They lacked the organization, leadership, ability or will to prevail against what remained one of the world's major powers. It was not the unarmed infidels but the now largely forgotten powerful Muslim elites—Bosnian beys, Hercegovinan *kapetans,* Albanian provincial governors, the warlord Pasvanoglu in the Danube port city of Vidin—who posed the most serious internal challenge to the Istanbul government in the Napoleonic era. Constant rebellions in mid-eighteenth-century Bosnia led the Sultan to talk about the "reconquest" of the province. Over time, matters got worse. "The Pachas, or Governors of provinces, are yet more independent of the Sultan than were the great Barons of the Crown in the feudal times of Christendom," wrote a British onlooker in June 1803. "Almost the whole extent of European Turkey presents a dreadful picture of anarchy, rebellion and barbarism."[6]

As the Sultan struggled to bring Pasvanoglu in the north under control, insubordinate local Muslim janissary officers next door in the tiny border Pashalik of Belgrade, just across the river from Habsburg lands, were also carving out new fiefdoms for themselves. "Of all the Janissaries of the empire," writes the nineteenth-century historian Leopold von Ranke, "none were more opposed to the Sultan than those at Belgrade." Aiming to establish their own power base, they mured the Sultan's representative, the vizier of Belgrade, for being pro-Christian, and then began to massacre his supporters among the Christian notables (*knezes*) as well. The latter took up arms in the name of the Sultan; self-defense rather than the dream of independence was what drove them on initially. But the Sultan hesitated to accept their support. To arm Christians against Muslims—however loyal the former, however rebellious the latter—was an uncomfortable notion for the Porte.[7]

When as a result, the Serbian *knezes* appealed for help to the Russians in 1806, they thereby turned what had basically been a local insurgency into a liberation struggle. The Russians treasured the loyalties of Orthodox Christians, but they did not want the Ottoman empire to break up and fall into Napoleon's hands. Moreover, once Napoleon invaded Russia, the Russians had their hands full, and a Turkish army regained control around Belgrade. Hence the First Serb Uprising ended in defeat, largely as a consequence of Great Power struggles in Europe. But it had taken the Ottoman empire nine years to put down a small border war against poorly armed and disorganized Christian farmers and traders. It was not a good omen, and it strengthened the modernizers' arguments in Istanbul for wholesale reform of the Ottoman state. Even worse was to follow.

Not all Serbs fled abroad like the insurrection's leader, Djordje Petrović (Karajordje). "How will it profit the Sultan to have an empty land?" reasoned one of the rebels, who decided to stay and to throw himself upon the mercy of Ottoman officials. "What will Serbia be worth if all the Serbs are slaughtered?" The wily Serb leader Miloš Obrenović also remained to serve the Sultan and was appointed grand knez in order to pacify the country. Two years later, he assumed the leadership of a second uprising. In the spring of 1815, he first conducted his Muslim blood brother, Aschin Bey, to safety, and then proclaimed the opening of a new "war against the Turks." Messages were sent around the country that the inhabitants should kill anyone they encountered wearing green clothes—the sign of a Muslim.[8]

On this occasion the Serbs' timing was better: Napoleon's defeat at Waterloo allowed the Russians to attend to their Balkan clients, and under Russian pressure the Turks were forced to make concessions to the Serbs. A Turkish garrison remained in Belgrade, but Muslims were confined to the towns of the Pachalik. In return for reaffirming his loyalty to the Sultan, Miloš became its de facto ruler. Governing the Serbs much as the pashas themselves had done, he sent the head of his political rival Karajordje to the Sultan, assassinated others who disputed his authority and hanged rebellious peasants. So far as the Porte was concerned, the arrangement bought peace in the tiny Pachalik at a time when far more serious challenges to Ottoman rule were afoot in Epirus and Bosnia, where well-armed local beys disputed the Sultan's authority. When the Greek revolt broke out, Miloš stood prudently aside to demonstrate his loyalty to the Porte. His reward came in 1828–1829, when another Russo-Turkish war led to further Ottoman concessions: his recognition as hereditary prince of Serbia, and complete internal autonomy. From this point on, it was possible to see Serbia as a separate state. But before 1878, when it won formal independence at the Congress of Berlin, it could also be viewed more ambiguously as an autonomous Christian principality within the Turkish empire—much like the Danubian Principalities or the newly formed Principality of Sámos, all of which offered forms of Christian self-government within the Ottoman domains. The ultimate triumph of the nation-state was still some way off.[9]

Perhaps the most formidable and durable of the Sultan's disobedient provincial governors in the early nineteenth century was the wily Ali Pasha, the venerable-looking but ruthless Albanian whose reach extended from his base in Jannina as far east as the Vardar River and as far south as the Gulf of Corinth. In the course of his lengthy struggle with the Porte, and amid complex double-dealings with British and French diplomats, Ali contemplated using the Greeks. He knew that a struggle for liberation had long been plotted in Greek revolutionary circles in Odessa, Vienna and elsewhere, and that the semisecret Friendly Society was laying the ground for insurrection. Ali spoke Greek, had a Greek Orthodox wife and employed Greek advisers who urged him to convert to Christianity and to whom he talked encouragingly of restoring the "empire of the Romans." Greek schools flourished in his capital, Jannina, which was an important center of Christian learning and education.[10]

In 1821 the Porte mounted a campaign to crush Ali and sent troops against him in Jannina. As this was going on, not one but two Greek uprisings took place, hundreds of miles apart. The first and less successful occurred in the Danubian lands, close to the thriving Greek world of the Black Sea. Its leader was a Phanariot and former Russian army general named Alexandros Ypsilantis. Russia had become a major source of support for the Greeks—a center of wealth, conspiracy and sympathy in high diplomatic circles. Ypsilantis himself had been an aide-de-camp to Tsar Alexander I; Ioannis Capodistrias, who turned down leadership of the insurgency and later became the first president of independent Greece, was an influential figure in Russian diplomatic circles. Writing from nearby Kishinev, Pushkin described how the Greeks

published proclamations which quickly spread everywhere—in them it is said that the Phoenix of Greece will arise from its own ashes, that the hour of Turkey's downfall has come, and that a great power approves of the great-souled feat! The Greeks have begun to throng together in crowds under three banners; of these one is tricolored, on another streams a cross wreathed with laurels, with the text "By this sign conquer" [God's promise to Constantine the Great], on a third is depicted the Phoenix arising from its ashes.[11]

Had Russia lent her support, as Ypsilantis had hoped, the Danubian uprising might have heralded the Byzantine imperial renaissance of which the Phanariots dreamed. But in fact the Tsar was anxious to preserve the peace in Europe. "The emperor has highly disapproved of those [means] which Prince Ipsilanti appears to wish to employ to deliver Greece," wrote Capodistrias to a friend. "At a time when Europe is menaced everywhere by revolutionary explosions, how can one not recognize in that which has broken out in the two principalities the identical effect of the same subversive principles, the same intrigues which attract the calamities of war...the most dreadful plague of demagogic despotism." The rebels were easily crushed by the Turkish army after Romanian peasants refused their support as well. "I am not prepared to shed Romanian blood for Greeks," stated the Romanian insurgent leader Tudor Vladimirescu. The main consequence of this failure was the collapse of Phanariot influence north of the Danube, and the eventual disappearance of an important center of Greek learning.[12]

A month later, as spring ushered in a new fighting season, a second Greek revolt occurred far to the south in the Peloponnese—where the peasantry were mostly Greek-speaking, and where a major insurrection had already taken place at Russian prompting in 1770, with bloody consequences. The eventual success of this rising rather than Ypsilantis's meant that when a Greek state did emerge, it was not as a new Byzantium spread across Europe and Anatolia, but as a modest little kingdom with a capital eventually based in the small

Ottoman market town of Athens. But success was far from assured there either.

At first, all eyes were on the struggle between the Porte and the rebellious and wily Ali Pasha to the north. In the Peloponnese port of Patras, Greeks were still hoping that the Muslim Albanian ruler of Jannina would "win and deliver them" from Ottoman rule. In fact, the local Ottoman authorities feared the same thing. Unwittingly they triggered off the Greek revolt by imprisoning those notables they could find as a preemptive move against Ali's Christian supporters. Faced with the choice of arrest or rebellion, many Greeks chose the latter and began to attack Muslim settlements. "The cloud of Darkness which overspread the Westward for so many a year, seems now to commence by casting its shadow of desolation and horror in this country," was how one British onlooker in Macedonia greeted news of the outbreak of revolt. "This revolutionary spirit of independence seems to gain in other parts of Greece also." Perhaps fifteen thousand of the forty thousand Muslim inhabitants of the Peloponnese were killed by insurgent bands in the first few months; survivors fled to the safety of towns and forts. That summer Greek forces besieged and eventually sacked the provincial capital of Tripolis. "The host which entered it," recollected one of the Greeks, "cut down and were slaying men, women and children from Friday until Sunday. Thirty two thousand were reported to have been slain.... About a hundred Greeks were killed; but the end came; a proclamation was issued that the slaughter must cease."[13]

At the end of 1821, the leaders of the Greek revolt met in assembly, proclaimed a constitution and appealed to Europe for help. Their sympathizers declared that Ottoman control of European territory was "an eternal shame to enlightened governments." But the Greeks—like the Serbs earlier—were disorganized and quarrelsome. They fought among themselves and frittered away their early successes; after 1825 a well-organized Turco-Egyptian invasion force laid waste to the Peloponnese. History would at this point merely have recorded one more failed insurgency had not Europe come to the rescue. Fearful that Ibrāhīm Pasha's army would enslave the Christians of the Peloponnese, George Canning, the British prime minister, warned that he "would not permit the execution of a system of depopulation." Ibrāhīm was told "to disavow or formally renounce ... the intention of converting the Morea [the Peloponnese] into a Barbary State by transporting the population to Asia and Africa and replacing them by the populations of those countries." Ottoman reprisals three years earlier on Chios, which had left thousands of Greeks dead and thousands more sold into slavery, had shocked the liberal conscience of Europe (and been immortalized by Delacroix). To keep an eye on the situation, the Great Powers sent a naval flotilla to the Peloponnese, which at the battle of Navarino destroyed the Turkish fleet. The Egyptian army then withdrew under the watchful gaze of a French expeditionary force. In this way, thanks largely to outside intervention, an independent Greek state was formed in 1830, and two years later the powers bestowed the youthful Prince Otto of Bavaria, a seventeen-year-old Catholic, upon the country as its king.[14]

Historians often explain why what happened had to happen. In the case of the rise of the Balkan nation-state, their grand explanatory schemes attribute the success of Christian nationalism to emergent merchant diasporas and the impact of Western ideology. None of this would have counted had it not been for Ottoman military and administrative weakness—especially at the empire's fringes—and the changing international balance of power. The Serbs were militarily defeated by 1810, the Greeks by 1827, but they won their statehood nonetheless. "It is doubtful," writes one scholar, "that the Serbs could have won independence from the Ottoman Empire without the full support of one or more major powers." The same was true for the Greeks. In both cases, the outcomes were tiny, insecure polities, pale shadows of the grand visions of resurrected empires whose prospect animated Balkan revolutionaries.

The dominant power in the region was still the Ottoman empire. After losing Greece (and Egypt), the Porte finally smashed the obstructive janissary corps, modernized its army and undertook a series of reforms. Ali Pasha was killed in 1822, the Bosnian beys were defeated in 1831 and the imperial state centralized its power. The reforms led to some efforts to reduce arbitrary oppression of Balkan Christians by local beys. "The *rayah* have hitherto sufficiently suffered," stated an Ottoman official in 1837, reproving landowners for forcing peasants to work on Sunday. "It is the will of the Sultan that they should be protected and allowed the full enjoyment of their religion."[15]

There was still life in the "Sick Man of Europe": Turkish troops defeated the Greek army in battle as late as 1897. There was economic vitality too: many Greeks and Serbs remained Ottoman citizens and showed little inclination to immigrate into their new "mother country"; some, on the contrary, fled the high tax rates and poor prospects of the new kingdom of Greece for Ottoman Anatolia or the ports of the Black Sea. The markets of the empire continued to attract Christian merchants, and Orthodox Christians still served the Porte as ambassadors and counselors.[16]

The two new states were impoverished, rural countries. Serbia was, in Lamartine's words, "an ocean of forests," with more pigs than humans. Serbian intellectual life in the Habsburg lands was far more advanced than in Belgrade. Perhaps 800,000 Greeks inhabited the new Greek kingdom, while more than 2 million still remained subjects of the Porte. No urban settlement in Greece came close to matching the sophistication and wealth of Ottoman cities such as Smyrna, Salonika and the capital itself. There were, to be sure, impressive signs of revitalization for those who wished to look: the rapidly expanding new towns built on modern grid patterns that replaced the old Ottoman settlements in Athens, Patras, Tripolis and elsewhere, for example, or the neoclassical mansions and public buildings commissioned by newly independent governments. "Some barracks, a hospital, a prison built on the model of our own," wrote Adolphe Blanqui from Belgrade in 1841, "announce the presence of an emergent civilization." In fact, similar trends of town planning and European architecture were transforming Ottoman cities as well.[17]

The inhabitants of the new states were as viciously divided among themselves in peace as they had been in war. In Serbia adherents of the Karajordje and Obrenović factions tussled for power, locals vied with the so-called Germans (Serb emigrants from the Habsburg lands), Turcophiles fought Russophiles. In Greece there were similar struggles between regional factions, between supporters of the various Great Powers, who each sponsored parties of their own, and between "autochthones" and "heterochthones." These divisions embittered politics from the start. The new states enjoyed liberty from Muslim rule but the pride they took at having won a place of their own in the world was tempered by a keen sense of inferiority vis-à-vis the powers. Nor did their triumph mean that people in the Balkans immediately started thinking in terms of nation-states. On the contrary, "Romania" and "Bulgaria" were notions that as late as 1830 animated only a handful of intellectuals and activists, "Albania" and "Macedonia" in all likelihood next to none. In southeastern Europe, far from the Nation winning itself an independent state—as romantic nationalists imagined—the leaders of new states had to create the Nation out of a peasant society that was imbued with the worldview of its Ottoman past. "Serbia," noted Blanqui, "owes to Miloš the first routes penetrating its forests, order re-established in its finances, the creation of Serbian nationality."[18]

———

The Danubian Principalities of Wallachia and Moldavia—the future Romania—were home to a miserably impoverished Romanian-speaking peasantry, ruled by an indigenous landowning boyar class and governed by Greek princes who owed allegiance to the Sultan. Fought over by Turkey and Russia for most of the eighteenth century, they were the most important example of those autonomous provinces that inhabited an intermediate space between total incorporation within the empire and independence. After the failure of the 1821 Greek revolt there, the decline of Phanariot power left the way open for the princes of the provinces to be elected from among the Romanian boyars themselves, an important step toward the creation of a native governing elite. The Porte was obliged to accept this change, thanks to Russian prodding, in 1826. In 1829, after a campaign that took its armies to within three days' march of Constantinople, Russia imposed military rule, although the provinces—like Serbia—remained nominally under the Sultan. According to the treaty of Adrianople, which marked the peace, the principalities were to "enjoy the free exercise of their worship, perfect security, an independent national government and full liberty of commerce."[19]

But the promise of national independence did not square with the reality of Russian military occupation. The modernizing Russian administrators, influenced by contemporary British and French theories of agrarian reform, intervened far more in the provinces' internal affairs than the Turks or the

Phanariots had done. The church was subjected to the state, as in Russia. Bucharest was transformed by town planners, acquiring numbered houses and street names (just two decades after Berlin), lighting and new drains. Like the Bavarians running Otto's kingdom of Greece, the Russians based their reforms upon theories of enlightened conservative bureaucracy. With the Organic Regulations of 1832, they introduced a cash economy into the landed estates, boosting grain production, formalizing the boyars' legal ownership of the land and exacerbating class tensions in the countryside.[20]

Before long, the Romanians' new masters were as unpopular as the old. In the revolutionary year of 1848, Russian and Turkish troops acted together to suppress liberal nationalist uprisings in Bucharest and Jassy. Like that of the Greeks before them, the Russians' influence among the Romanians waned, and the latter began to embrace Latinism—in particular, the culture of their Latin "sister nation," France. French replaced Greek in fashionable circles and was used in official bulletins. Some dreamed of turning Bucharest, the capital of Wallachia, into the "Paris of the Balkans."[21]

After Russia's defeat in the Crimean War, the French encouraged the idea of a union of the two principalities as a barrier to further Tsarist penetration toward Constantinople. French support and smart maneuvering by local Romanian elites brought this about. In 1859, the two provincial assemblies elected the same man, Alexandru Cuza, "a card player who preferred Jamaica rum to public affairs," as ruler, and the two assemblies voted for unification. In this strange way, Romania came into existence (even so, it had to wait till 1878 for formal international recognition). Cuza's reign—like that of most rulers of the new Balkan states—was brief, though he at least avoided assassination. He made enemies among the landowners by his agrarian reforms and was pushed from power in 1866. As in Greece earlier, local elites failed to accept a native head of state, and a monarchical house had to be imported from abroad. Prince Karl of Hohenzollern-Sigmaringen, a cousin of the king of Prussia, was said never to have heard of Romania before his nomination as its king. Nevertheless, like his contemporary King George of Greece (a "good boy but not overbright and a very plain youth" was Queen Victoria's comment), as King Carol I, he enjoyed a long and successful reign, until his death in 1914.

———

The emergence of Bulgaria was relatively late—in the wake of the last Russian invasion into Ottoman Europe, in 1877—and highly contentious. Despite the presence of a small Bulgarian intelligentsia and a nationalist cultural and economic revival during the nineteenth century, proximity to Constantinople had made it relatively easy for the Turks and the patriarchate between them to control the Bulgarian Slavs. A peasant uprising in 1841 had been ruthlessly and effectively crushed by Albanian irregulars, and many Bulgarians had fled northward to the Danubian Principalities, to Russia and later to Serbia; what little revolutionary conspiracy as there was took place in the coffee shops and inns of Bucharest and Jassy. Armed Bulgarian bands who crossed the Danube were easily crushed by Ottoman troops. Bulgarian notables were mostly pro-Greek in culture and loyal to the Sultan. When the Russian scholar Yuri Venelin visited Bulgaria in 1830 to collect materials for his pioneering historical and ethnographic studies of the Bulgarian people, he found them apathetic and unresponsive to his inquiries. It was scarcely clear what it meant to call oneself Bulgarian. "Even forty years ago," wrote an observer in 1900, "the name Bulgarian was almost unknown and every educated person coming from that country called himself Greek as a matter of course."[22]

Disillusioned at the lack of patriotic feeling among peasants and merchants and at the failure of their efforts at armed insurrection, Bulgarian revolutionaries turned to nonmilitant strategies, and dreamed of creating an autonomous Christian–Orthodox confederation to share power with the Sultan. Hungary's success in creating the Dual Monarchy out of the Habsburg empire in 1867 exemplified the benefits of a peaceful struggle. And for a moment, reform seemed possible under the Porte too: many Bulgarians lived in the model Danube *vilayet*, run by the reformist Midhat Pasha, who appointed Christian officials on an equal footing—at least in theory—with Muslims. But most of these Christians were in fact Polish, Hungarian and Croat émigrés rather than Bulgarians; and Midhat himself was replaced after three years, victim of the perennial instability inside the Ottoman administration.[23]

Religious changes did more than patriotic activism to shape an emergent Bulgarian consciousness. American Protestant missionaries translated the New Testament into a language Bulgarian peasants could understand, and thereby began to erode the dominance of Greek. Even so, the missionaries found that so few peasants could read their own language that they seriously contemplated printing Bibles instead in Turkish written in Slavonic characters. In 1849, following pressure from Bulgarian guilds in Constantinople, a Bulgarian church was consecrated in the grounds of the home of the remarkable Stefan Bogoridi—a counselor to the Sultan, prince of Sámos, and partly Bulgarian by origin. Further agitation against Greek dominance in the patriarchate, and against the exactions of Greek bishops in the countryside, led to the establishment of a separate Bulgarian church in 1870. Yet for long thereafter there were many Bulgarian-speaking peasants (as would become clear in Macedonia) who considered themselves Greeks—by which they meant not that they supported the expansionist schemes of the kingdom of Greece to the south, but that they worshiped in churches run by the patriarchate. A sense that speaking Bulgarian implied belonging to a Bulgarian nation was slow to emerge.[24]

In 1876 the latest in a line of Bulgarian revolts failed to elicit support among the peasantry or townspeople. "The April Uprising," writes B. Jelavich, "which became the major event in later Bulgarian nationalist mythology, was a complete failure as a revolution." Europe was not much preoccupied by the one hundred or so Turkish civilians killed by the rebels. However, the Sultan, who was engaged by a serious insurrection in the western Balkans, was alarmed at another insurgency so close to the center of the empire and ordered its swift and brutal suppression. News of the "Bulgarian horrors" committed by Ottoman irregulars—with perhaps 12,000 to 15,000 Christians killed—attracted European concern, and even became the focus of a British electoral campaign. When the Sultan rejected European calls for internal reform, Russia invaded the Balkans in 1877, and after encountering surprisingly stiff Turkish resistance, eventually advanced on Constantinople. The peace terms dictated to the Turks that year established independence for Romania, Serbia and Montenegro, and thus marked the end of Ottoman Europe as it had existed for centuries. But the clause that created the greatest stir was the establishment of a vast new autonomous Bulgarian state, which would have extended westward to Skopje and the Vardar valley, and south to Salonika and the Aegean. This was the so-called San Stefano Bulgaria, named after the treaty that gave it birth.[25]

San Stefano Bulgaria did not last more than a few months. The other powers, above all Britain, saw it as an unacceptable extension of Russian power into the Balkans. At the Congress of Berlin in 1878, Disraeli insisted that the new Bulgarian state be whittled down to an area less than half the size of that originally envisaged. Macedonia was returned to Ottoman rule, and a new area, the autonomous province of Eastern Rumelia, was created between Bulgaria and Constantinople. This province was soon annexed to Bulgaria, and it took a mere thirty years for the country to move from being an autonomous principality paying tribute to the Sultan to full independence. But Bulgarians never forgot the state the Russians had originally promised them, and the "lost lands" of Macedonia in particular became the object of their dreams of expansion.

———

The process of nation building in the Balkans occupied the entire nineteenth century. It was protracted and experimental and left many of the region's "little people" still subjects of imperial power, whether under the Ottomans or—as in the case of the Croats, Slovenes, Serbs, Romanians and others—under the Habsburgs. Still, autonomy turned out not to be an alternative to full national independence, as many federalists inside and outside the Ottoman empire had hoped, but the preliminary to it: the passage from autonomy to independence took over a century in the case of the Danubian Principalities, decades for Serbia and Bulgaria, and less than three years for Greece. Crete and Sámos, which also won autonomy within the empire, became part of Greece before the First World War.

The Great Powers were heavily involved in the new states' internal affairs. They appointed their kings from the unemployed scions of Europe's princely houses, drew up their constitutions and selected teams of military and civilian advisers—from the Bavarians who ran Greece under King Otto in the 1840s to the Russians who ran Bulgaria, including its army and Ministry of War, in the 1880s. They defined borders and adjusted territories at diplomatic conferences and imposed their wishes on all parties through gunboat diplomacy and economic arm-twisting. Yet their control of the new states was not assured—as the Russians found in Romania and Bulgaria, and the Austrians in Serbia. The Great Powers had yielded to the forces of nationalism and created independent states. But thereafter they tried to preserve what remained of the Ottoman empire. What thwarted their efforts was the strength of expansionism as a major focus for popular politics in the countries they had themselves created. Here lay the fundamental instability of the new situation in the Balkans.

The sense of mission in Balkan politics was driven by the dream of territorial expansion. All states could point to "unredeemed" brethren or historic lands that lay outside the boundaries apportioned them by the powers: Romanians in Hungarian Transylvania; Serbs in Habsburg Croatia and Ottoman lands; Bulgarians in the lands of the San Stefano state they had been cheated of; Greeks—in thrall to the "Great Idea" of a new Byzantine empire—redeeming hellenism across the Ottoman empire from Crete to the Black Sea. Popular irredentism mobilized public opinion, financed cross-border incursions by bands of irregulars and often forced unwilling Balkan monarchs into rash adventures against the advice or wishes of the powers. Milan Obrenović was pushed against his own inclinations into declaring war on Turkey in 1876 to support insurgent Orthodox Christians in Bosnia, and in 1885 he invaded Bulgaria. Neither adventure was a success, and on both occasions the Serbs were saved further humiliation only by Great Power intervention. Greeks mounted a series of failed invasions of Ottoman lands from 1854 to 1897; the 1922 Asia Minor disaster was the last of a series of ill-thought-through Greek military expeditions, which were subsequently blamed on lack of support from the powers.[26]

But if the Balkan states overestimated their own irredentist capacities, the Great Powers failed to take them seriously enough. They had a low opinion of their new creations and often treated them as puppets. For Count Grula Andrássy, the Austro-Hungarian foreign minister, in 1873, Austria's Near Eastern neighbors were "wild Indians who could only be treated like unbroken horses, to whom corn should be offered with one hand while they are threatened with a whip in the other." Archduke Franz Ferdinand himself described Serbia as a land of "thieves and murderers and bandits and a few plum trees." After the Habsburg army occupied Ottoman Bosnia in 1878, thereby acquiring a long new border with Serbia, diplomats at Vienna believed they had checked Serbian expansion and had the corrupt Obrenovićs in their pocket. But Balkan public opinion resented subservience to the powers, and monarchs who behaved too much like puppets of powerful neighbors were likely to end up like Alexander Obrenović, who was murdered in 1903 by Serbian army officers and replaced by his rival, the less slavishly Austrophile King Peter.

Russia too believed that it enjoyed an unshakable grip on Slavic loyalties. Yet even though Romania and Bulgaria owed their very existence to Russia, both quickly came to resent the interference of their great northern neighbor. Perhaps the clearest expression of Russian overconfidence occurred in 1912: Russian diplomats encouraged the Balkan states to band together in the Balkan League to put pressure on Austria-Hungary. In fact the league turned instead on Turkey, driving it out of Europe—something the Russians had not bargained for—before turning on itself and splitting up. Neither Slavic nor Orthodox solidarity was ever as powerful a factor in Balkan–Russian relations as nervous Westerners feared.

If 1878 was the high point of Great Power control over the Balkans, the next thirty years marked the breakdown. European stability was ensured so long as Austria and Russia enjoyed good relations with each other. Under Bismarck,

Germany acted as broker between the two, and the alliance of these three powers closed off the possibility of Balkan politicians exploiting any rivalry between them. But Bismarck departed the scene in 1890, and his successors in Berlin were increasingly anti-Russian. Austria itself looked toward the lands of the South Slavs as other major powers carved up Africa and expanded their empires overseas. Even so, in 1897, Austria and Russia reached an agreement to "eliminate the danger of a rivalry disastrous to the peace of Europe on the seething soil of the Balkan peninsula." At this time, Russian foreign policy was turned toward the Far East rather than the Balkans. Only after its 1905 defeat by Japan would Russia return to southeastern Europe, and the tension with Austria-Hungary turn sour. The point of conflict was the heart of what remained of Ottoman Europe—Macedonia.

———

Macedonia was a region with no clear borders and not even a formal existence as an administrative Ottoman entity. A bewildering mix of different peoples, hemmed in by newly created states (Greece to the south, Serbia and Bulgaria to the north) it became the focus for their expansionist ambitions at the century's close. Its ethnography, however, posed a challenge for the most ardent Balkan nationalist and had changed out of all recognition since the days of Alexander the Great. The peasantry of the region were predominantly Orthodox, and mostly Slavs; Greek speakers fringed coastal areas and inhabited the towns. The capital, Salonika, which one commentator called the "coveted city," was a typical polyglot Ottoman port whose bootblacks could make themselves understood in half a dozen languages, but it had one unique feature: of the ethnic kaleidoscope that made up its population, the largest single group were not Greeks, Turks, Albanians or Slavs but Sephardic Jews. Inside and outside the city, no single ethnic group prevailed. Nationalism could offer a basis for rule over such a land only with the aid of extreme violence and a good deal of wishful thinking.

"In one sense," wrote the British diplomat Sir Charles Eliot in 1900, "a race in Macedonia is merely a political party." The struggle for the loyalties of the Slav Orthodox peasantry was waged between pro-Greek and pro-Bulgarian factions. Both sides founded schools to propagate their national ideals, established churches loyal to "their" bishops, produced maps and ethnographies to justify their claim and financed armed bands of patriots—some local, some supported by outside agents—to gain peasant adherents to their cause where more peaceful methods could not be guaranteed to bring success. Serbs and Romanians also propagandized, though more halfheartedly. The Greeks took a while to organize themselves, while the Bulgarians were weakened by a murderous split in their own ranks between those who fought for a Greater Bulgaria, and the members of the Internal Macedonian Revolutionary Organization (IMRO), who wanted autonomy for Macedonia. For the most part, the Turkish authorities sat back and watched the Christians fight among themselves, occasionally sending in Albanian irregulars when matters threatened to boil over.[27]

Ethnicity was as much the consequence as the cause of this unrest; revolutionary violence produced national affiliations as well as being produced by them. The unfortunate peasants themselves were concerned more to regain some stability in their lives than to die for nationalism. "Our fathers were Greeks and none mentioned the Bulgarians," confessed one. "We became Bulgarians, we won. If we have to be Serbs, no problem. But for now it is better for us to be Bulgarians." Caught between hard-line revolutionaries and the unpredictably repressive Ottoman state, many immigrated—to Bulgaria, Greece, central Europe or across the Atlantic. Those who remained were pawns in a political struggle between sides that were relying increasingly on violence to secure their loyalty.[28]

When pro-Bulgarian activists organized a rising at Djumaya to which local villagers reacted with indifference, the latter were rewarded by having their homes burned down by the Ottoman authorities and their cattle sold off. The following spring, IMRO bombed targets in Salonika and in the autumn unleashed the Ilinden revolt, this time triggering off a larger peasant uprising and another Turkish reprisal. Their purpose, like that of so many insurrectionaries before and since, was to embroil the Great Powers on the side of their demands for autonomy. But in this they failed: for the last time, the Russian Tsar Nicholas II and Austro-Hungarian Emperor Franz Josef were able to agree upon a reform program for the Ottoman province.[29]

These Murzsteg reforms were the last real cooperation between the two major powers involved in the Balkans. Austria was alarmed by Serbia's assertiveness after the murder of the pro-Austrian King Alexander Obrenović. When Serbia and Bulgaria established a secret customs union in 1905, the Austrians made them dissolve it. The following year there was a new quarrel after the Serbs purchased arms in France rather than from the Habsburg empire. In the "Pig War" the Austrians again tried to coerce the Serbs, this time through economic sanctions. Given that 80 to 90 percent of Serbian exports went via the empire, the Serbs might have been expected to knuckle under. Instead they rerouted their trade south and moved closer to Russia. The Austrians began to fear, in Sorel's words, that "when the Eastern Question appears to have been resolved, Europe will inevitably face the Austrian question." In the middle of the nineteenth century, the small independent state of Piedmont had created Italy by taking over the Habsburgs' Italian provinces; now Vienna feared that Serbia might do the same thing with the empire's South Slavs.

In 1908 reformist army officers in Macedonia, angry at Ottoman weakness and continued Western intervention, led a revolt against the Porte. When Sultan Abdul Hamid II declared that he was restoring the 1876 Ottoman constitution, a wave of euphoria swept the province and it looked as if the empire might transform itself under the revolutionaries into a multiethnic state with religious equality and civic rights for all. In Macedonia there was a brief moment of celebration. "The Mullahs offered up prayers, the Greek bishop and representatives of the League of Union and Progress made speeches," came the reports from one town in July. "Officers and civilians have been haranguing the crowd from the steps of the government buildings," reported a British diplomat in Salonika, the center of the revolt, on July 23. "They speak in favor of liberty and representative government and assert that the Constitution has already been formally proclaimed."[30]

But there were those who had reason not to welcome the salvation of the Ottoman empire. The Ottoman dynasty feared that reform would be more likely to lose it support among its Muslim population than to win it among Christians. When Abdul Hamid first traveled by train, the reaction of Muslim bystanders had been scathing: "The Padishah has become a *giaour* [Christian]." Like railways, constitutionalism marked the disruptive intrusion of Christian values into the hierarchal world of Ottoman Islam. Equally fearful, however, of this constitutional revolution was Austria-Hungary, which had occupied the Ottoman province of Bosnia-Hercegovina in 1878. Worried lest the Young Turks try to extend voting rights there, Vienna moved quickly to annex the province outright.[31]

At least one Habsburg expert on the South Slavs saw trouble ahead. To many Bosnian peasants in 1908, the Habsburg emperor was still "our old father" (*stari otac*). But this traditional deference to dynastic authority was waning. The roads, railways and schools the Austrians were building in their new province facilitated the spread of Serbian nationalism among the Bosnian Orthodox. And Serb nationalism was linked to the agrarian question. While peasants were free in Croatia, Hungary and Serbia, in Bosnia-Hercegovina four fifths awaited emancipation and existed under an Ottoman feudal order preserved by the Austrians. "Plainly no one has ever stopped to consider the impression bound to be made...on the minds of a population which knows that across the Drina and Sava rivers, there is no sub-pasha to appropriate a third of the harvest every year for Beg or Aga." Habsburg efforts to inculcate a sense of Bosnian nationhood had failed.[32]

The only alternative seemed to save Bosnia for the empire by "placing the center of the South Slav world inside Austria." Throughout the nineteenth century, Hungary's increasingly autocratic rule over Serbs and Croats had provoked the emergence of a movement for South Slav cooperation. Bishop Josip Strossmayer, a member of the Vienna Reichsrat, was among those who sought to build closer ties among Serbs, Croats and Slovenes, and through institutions such as the Yugoslav Academy and Zagreb University laid the foundations for a movement that might win rights for the South Slavs within the Habsburg system. But even inside the empire this policy encountered the adamant opposition of the Hungarians, who did not wish to share power with the South Slavs.

Outside the empire, the Serbs saw themselves as a Balkan Piedmont with a mission to free the remaining South Slavs from captivity. They interpreted Austria-Hungary's annexation of Bosnia as a move against them. The Russians too opposed it, especially as they knew the Austrians wanted to construct a railroad southward to the Aegean. A British diplomat commented, "The struggle between Austria and Russia in the Balkans is evidently now beginning." Both Russia and Serbia demanded compensation from the Austrians, but neither got it. The Serbs expected Russian support, even to the point of a declaration of war against Austria. "All think of revenge which is only to be carried out with the help of the Russians," the Austrian ambassador reported from Belgrade. But the Russians backed down when Berlin warned that Germany would mobilize in turn in support of Vienna. "Russia is not yet ready with her army and cannot now make war," the Russian foreign minister informed the Serbs. In 1914, they would receive a different answer.[33]

In Serbia and Bosnia itself secret societies sprang up opposed to Habsburg rule—among them Union or Death, the organization implicated in the Sarajevo shooting in 1914. Serb success in the Balkan wars turned "what was only a hope a year ago," reported an Austrian observer of pro-Serb sentiment in Bosnia in October 1913, into "a deep-rooted political movement." The dilemma for Austria-Hungary sharpened. "We have got either to annihilate Serbia or, if we cannot do that, learn to love it," commented one analyst. The assassination of Franz Ferdinand led the Austrian government to take the road to the first alternative, and unleashed an almost identical sequence of events to that of 1908; in 1914, however, the Russians felt they could not back down a second time. Hence Europe's second Bosnian crisis led to its First World War.[34]

But by then the map of the Balkans had already been drastically altered by the almost total collapse of Ottoman power in Europe. The Young Turk revolution, far from reconciling Balkan subjects to Ottoman rule, had hastened the empire's disintegration. As the Habsburg empire was also to find, nationalism dissolved the old imperial bonds. Turkish nationalism—which was the basis on which the revolutionaries of the Committee of Union and Progress hoped to modernize the empire—simply increased Christian emnity. By 1911 there were more than two hundred guerrilla bands operating in Macedonia and the outlook was grimmer than for many years.

In particular, the government's efforts to modernize the Ottoman state alienated the one people traditionally loyal to the regime, the Albanians. Christians and Muslims, they had served the Sultan as irregular soldiers and bodyguards, their loyalty secured by the Porte's willingness to allow them arms and autonomy. Edith Durham, a sympathetic observer, described villages whose men "when called on for military service ... will often declare themselves Christians and exempt, and afterward repel with guns the men sent to collect army tax on the grounds that they are Moslems and not liable." In 1910 an uprising in northern Albania was defeated only with the aid of 20,000 Ottoman troops. And the next year—as Italy went to war with the Ottoman empire in Libya and contemplated an invasion of Albania—an even larger revolt saw the rebels call for the first time for the recognition of Albania as a separate nation and for virtual self-government. "The formation of a commission at Dibra to consider a demand for the recognition of Albanians in official registers as 'Albanians' and not as 'Moslems' or 'non-Moslems' is especially significant," noted the British ambassador in Constantinople. "The notables forming the commission are apparently themselves Moslems and that they should even consider a proposal to demand a national instead of a religious status is an entirely new and very remarkable development."[35]

The Albanian rebellion presaged radical changes in the balance of power in the Balkans. It showed that armed revolt against the Turkish authorities could succeed, spurring the Balkan states to assert their own claims to Ottoman territory. It marked the emergence of organized and militant Albanian nationalism, to the intense alarm of Serbia and Greece, both of which claimed territories with substantial Albanian-speaking populations. And it encouraged both Austria-Hungary and Italy to dream of new footholds in southeastern Europe, which alarmed the Balkan states still more.

In March 1912, therefore, Serbia and Bulgaria agreed to "unite in defense of their independence and integrity and in opposition to any attempt by a great power to invade the Balkan territories of the Ottoman empire." Greece and Montenegro soon joined them. Russian diplomats believed they had fostered a defensive bloc against Austria, but they woke up too late to see the Balkan League attack Turkey. "Russia tries to put on the brake," observed French Prime Minister Raymond Poincaré, "but it is she who has started the motor." "For the first time in the history of the Eastern Question," noted another French diplomat, "the small states have acquired a position of such independence of the Great Powers that they feel able to act completely without them and even to take them in tow."[36]

In the First Balkan War of 1912, Ottoman power in Europe vanished in a matter of weeks. Serbia and Greece were the main victors, both acquiring huge new territories. Bulgaria won much less, and was soon even worse off after she declared war on her former allies in the Second Balkan War the following year and was defeated by them. An independent Albania was recognized by the Great Powers, and defended against its hungry neighbors. The biggest loser in many ways—apart from the Ottoman empire—was Austria-Hungary, which now faced a successful and expansionist Serbia. Austria tried to build up Albania as a counterweight but could not prevent Kosovo and neighboring lands being assigned to Serbia and Montenegro.

The truth was that after two Balkan wars, Serbia was in no condition for a third. But in Vienna, that summer of 1914, many believed the time was ripe to crush Serbia once and for all. They knew they had the Germans behind them. On the other hand, the events of the 1908 Bosnian crisis made it virtually certain the Russians would back the Serbs, since they could not afford to lose face a second time. Hence the powers were bound to collide. After the assassination of the Archduke in Sarajevo, the Serbian government made almost all the concessions the Austrians demanded. It was not enough. The third Balkan war in three years was started by Austria; within a week, thanks to the system of obligations imposed by the rival alliances of Europe, all the Great Powers had become embroiled, and the conflict became continental in scope.

Taken in isolation, there was little reason that the breakdown of the Austro-Russian entente in the decades after 1878 should have led to war. After all, Austrian and Russian interests lay on opposite sides of the Balkan peninsula. But both powers felt weaker as time went on. The growth of Balkan nationalism and the power vacuum created by the decline of Ottoman authority made it difficult for them to secure vital interests—South Slav obedience in Habsburg domains; control of the Black Sea and access to the Mediterranean in the case of Russia. They needed local allies and proxies and were thus drawn into the confused politics of the region. Matters were not helped by their lack of judgment in handling these allies, whose military and diplomatic skills they often underestimated. Balkan states were practiced in the "politics of oscillation." In 1914, not for the last time in Balkan relations with the powers, the tail ended up wagging the dog.

———

Hajduks, klephts, *armatoles* and brigands were heroes in the Balkan nationalist pantheon. Their exploits were the stuff of legend and oral epic. The prosaic reality was that conventional military and naval forces were more important in determining political outcomes. The 160,000 troops launched by Russia across the Danube in 1877 did more than any *hajduks* or klephts to win freedom for Balkan Christians. Over the two centuries leading to the NATO intervention in Kosovo in 1999, regular armies would always win out over irregulars; the latter could prevail only by obtaining in turn the backing of a more powerful military force. The two Balkan wars of 1912–1913 demonstrated how far all the armies of the Balkans had adapted to the requirements of modern war. The arms race between them lasted right up to 1914. The Ottoman army was reorganized with Western advice and was led by Polish and Hungarian émigrés as well as British, American and German soldiers of fortune (like Mehmet Ali Pasha, a delegate at the Congress of Berlin, who had originally been a soldier in the Prussian army before converting and becoming an Ottoman army commander). Balkan armies too imported Western expertise and weaponry, huge investments for poor new states.

Regular armies bore the brunt of the fighting that followed as well. In 1914 the Serbs had a staggering 450,000 men under arms. By 1916, their strength was below 150,000, and 100,000 men had been killed. After two extraordinarily incompetent Habsburg invasions, and stiff resistance, the Serbian army was eventually forced to retreat to the sea, and abandon the country to military occupation. Turkey entered the war on the German side, and the other Balkan states saw an opportunity for what Bulgarian Foreign Minister Todorov described as "extortion," demanding territory in any future peace settlement in return for entering the war. Bulgaria took the side of the Central Powers in return for pledges of Serbian and Greek territory, and eventually mobilized 800,000 men.

Greece and Romania took longer before backing what turned out to be the right horse. In Romania, the government entered on the Triple Entente side in the summer of 1916 before quickly succumbing to the Central Powers. "To make the Romanian army fight a modern war," complained a Russian commander, "was asking a donkey to perform a minuet." Romania was better at bargaining than fighting. Within months, the Romanian army was dissolved and a pro-German government was installed in Bucharest. "Romanian intervention," according to Norman Stone, "made possible the German continuation of the war into 1918." Luckily for the Romanians, other armies were better than theirs, a fact that enabled the country to profit handsomely from the Paris Peace Conference.[37]

In Greece, pro- and anti-interventionists split the country into two before the former, led by Prime Minister Eleuthérios Venizélos, prevailed. Greek, Serbian, Italian, British and French forces—the so-called Gardeners of Salonika—occupied the Macedonian front against the Central Powers. In the autumn of 1918, the Triple Entente forces made a breakthrough there with a successful offensive. Indeed, it was the Bulgarian collapse at the end of September that led German military leaders to conclude that the war was lost. David Lloyd George, one of Britain's leading "Easterners," commented bitterly: "Unfortunately, just as there were many who found it unimaginable that events in the Balkans could start a world war, so there were those who refused to believe that events in such an obscure part of the world could end one."[38]

In fact, although the First World War ended in 1918, fighting in southeastern Europe continued for some time. The Ottoman empire had begun to disintegrate long before any of Europe's other multinational empires, but its final collapse came well after the Habsburgs and Romanovs had left their thrones. In 1919 Greek forces landed in Asia Minor. Having secured the backing of the Great Powers for a bridgehead around the city of Smyrna, Venizélos himself saw this as the chance to fulfill the irredentist "Great Idea" and to re-create a Byzantine empire based in Constantinople. But Greece's Asia Minor adventure ended in disaster: Turkish forces pushed the Greeks back to the Mediterranean coast, and eventually off the mainland altogether; Anatolia's large Orthodox population was put to flight. Out of the fighting of 1921–1922 emerged the modern republic of Turkey, under the leadership of Mustafa Kemal, better known as Atatürk. The last Ottoman sultan, Mehmed VI, fled Constantinople on a British battleship and died in San Remo in 1926, with debts so heavy that his creditors delayed his burial for two weeks. Meanwhile, Atatürk began the uphill task—which continues to this day—of turning the former heartland of the empire into a Turkish nation-state.[39]

"The Allied powers," stated the British foreign secretary in June 1915, "hope that as a result of the war, the political balance in the Balkans will be established on a broader and more national basis." The eventual outcome was more ambiguous than this. The compulsory population exchange of 1923 between Greece and Turkey—by which Muslims left Greece for Turkey, and Orthodox Anatolians "returned" to Greece—increased the ethnic homogeneity of both countries. Greek Macedonia, in which Greeks had been less than half the population before 1914, thereby became nearly 90 percent Greek. Jewish Salonika became Greek Thessaloniki with the resettlement of thousands of refugees from Asia Minor. Romania, on the other hand, which made huge territorial gains at the expense of former Russian and Habsburg lands, gained new minorities: by 1922, the country was one third larger than before the war, but only two thirds ethnically Romanian: Hungarian, Jewish and Ukrainian populations were all substantial.[40]

Above all, there was the unique case of the Kingdom of the Serbs, Croats and Slovenes, the state created at Versailles that would be better known by its later name of Yugoslavia. At the start of the war, none of the Triple Entente powers intended to dismember the Austro-Hungarian empire to create a "new Europe." Moreover, few South Slavs aspired to this either. But the collapse of the Habsburg empire and the threat from Italy, which had territorial demands of its own in Dalmatia, left the Croats and Slovenes with little choice but to embrace South Slav union under the leadership of Serbia's Karajordje dynasty. Suspicions that what they were getting was not federalism but centralized rule from Belgrade and Greater Serbia were alive from the start: there were tensions during the wartime discussions among Serb, Croat and Slovene leaders and armed resistance to incorporation in the new state after 1918 among peasants from Croatia to Montenegro. The 1921 constitution confirmed their worst fears: henceforth, Serb civil servants and army officers dominated the new Yugoslav state.[41]

By 1923, the Eastern Question had come to an end. A decade of wars had finally destroyed the empires that had ruled the Balkans, and much of eastern Europe, for centuries. But the collapse of empires did not bring the peace anticipated by Western liberals. The successor states appealed to the principle of nationality to claim their neighbors' lands: irredentism lived on, and few Balkan borders were uncontested. Moreover, the nationality principle cut two ways. All the new states had ethnic minorities whose existence undermined their claims to rule in the name of the Nation. Nor did Europe's Great Powers succeed after 1918 in patching up the differences that had led them into war. On the contrary, their rivalries were now sharpened and intensified by ideology as fascism and communism took hold. Thus the twentieth century, like the nineteenth, was scarred by the bloody intersection of regional Balkan quarrels and Great Power competitiveness. The era of religion was over; that of ideology lay ahead: nationalism spanned them both.

4

BUILDING THE NATION-STATE

We strained like eagles high above the clouds and now we roll
in the dust, in the swamp...! If this is the life a free people leads,
then such freedom is in vain. We sowed roses,
but only thorns have come forth.

—MIKHALAKI GEORGIEV[1]

"The claim to set up new States according to the limits of nationality is the most dangerous of all Utopian schemes," the Austrian Foreign Ministry warned in 1853. "To put forward such a pretension is to break with history; and to carry it into execution in any part of Europe is to shake to its foundations the firmly organized order of States, and to threaten the Continent with subversion and chaos." Within half a century, the new nation-states of the Balkans had defeated the Ottoman empire; by 1918 the Habsburgs had gone too. The order of European states established at the Congress of Vienna had been superseded by that of Versailles. But as the Hungarian historian Oscar Jaszi observed in a 1925 essay on "The Irresistibility of the National Idea," the First World War did not solve the nationality problem, since the right of self-determination could not as a matter of practical politics be extended to every national group. Indeed, the existence of both Yugoslavia and Czechoslovakia testified to the continuation of alternative forms of statehood. In the ethnic kaleidoscope of the Balkans, above all, the principle of nationality was a recipe for violence.[2]

For Ottoman Muslims, the repercussions of Christian triumph in southeastern Europe had long been evident. After the Habsburg conquest of Hungary and Croatia at the end of the seventeenth century, traces of Muslim life and monuments there were eradicated. In 1826 the powers agreed that so far as Greece was concerned, "In order to effect a complete separation between Individuals of the two Nations, and to prevent collisions which be necessary consequences of a contest of such a duration, the Greeks should purchase the property of Turks." In 1830, the Turks were ordered to withdraw from the Serbian countryside into garrison towns, and thirty years later it was agreed that all Turks not in these towns were to be deported and their property sold.[3]

In 1876–1878, a new wave of refugees moved across the Ottoman–Serbian border after fighting around Niš led to the expansion of Serb territory. Tens of thousands of Muslim Tartars and Circassians fled Bulgaria when the Russian army invaded in 1877; others were massacred by Russian troops and Christian peasants. Thessaly, an Ottoman province, had around 45,000 Muslim inhabitants when annexed by Greece in 1881; by 1911 there were only 3,000 left. In Crete, the Muslim population dropped from 73,000 in 1881 to 27,850 in 1911. Some fled to avoid war, others to escape persecution by bands or civilians or simply such humiliations as having to serve in armies under Christian officers. Organized official exchanges of population—which would become a feature of twentieth-century Balkan politics—were as yet unknown. When the Ottoman authorities proposed an exchange of Turkish and Bulgarian populations in 1878, the idea was rejected.[4]

But the problem of nationality went beyond the reversal of fortune faced by Balkan Muslims. The liberal concept of the nation-state aimed to reconcile majoritarian ethnic rule with guarantees of individual rights. The tension between these two elements had already been evident in the struggles over the nineteenth-century Romanian constitution, which—to the anger of the Great Powers—was clearly designed to exclude Jews from citizenship in the new state. In theory, assimilation of the minority to the majority was supposed in the long run to lead to a homogenization of the population. But the theory collided with the realities of politics in Europe's postimperial states, where tensions, animosities and suspicion among ethnic groups ran high.[5]

The decade of wars between 1912 and 1922 illuminated the scale of the problem. There had been many victims of the clash between Greek and Bulgarian bands in Ottoman Macedonia. But the numbers were far fewer than the civilian casualties of regular armies during the Balkan wars. In 1912, for the first time in the history of the region, modern states took advantage of a military conflict to pursue long-range demographic goals. In the former Ottoman districts of Kosovo and Monastir, in particular, the conquering Serb army killed perhaps thousands of civilians. Despite some Serb officers' careless talk of "exterminating" the Albanian population, this was killing prompted more by revenge than genocide. Still, the shootings appalled eyewitnesses and investigators. "The Turks are fleeing before the Christians, the Bulgarians before the Greeks and the Turks, the Greeks and Turks before the Bulgarians, the Albanians before the Servian," noted the investigating Carnegie Commission in 1914. "The means employed by the Greek against the Bulgarian, by the Turk against the Slav, by the Servian against the Albanian, is no longer extermination or emigration; it is an indirect method which must, however, lead to the same end, that of conversion and assimilation." Forced conversions, mass executions and the flight of tens of thousands of refugees were the consequence of this attempt to liquidate the remaining Ottoman provinces in Europe in accordance with the principle of nationality.[6]

Civilians in the Balkans continued to be viewed with suspicion by military forces during the First World War. In Kosovo, the struggle between Serbs and Albanians raged unchecked. The Bulgarian occupation of Macedonia and southern Serbia was brutal enough to provoke uprisings. But it was not just the Balkan peoples themselves who were involved: the imperial powers too were behaving more repressively than in the past. On October 8, 1914, for instance, the Austrian politician Josef Redlich recorded in his diary a visit from a Hungarian journalist, Josef Diner-Denes, who described a "race war" [*Rassenkrieg*] directed by the Habsburg authorities against the Serbs in southern Hungary. "Hundreds of Serbs have been interned, many of them innocent people." A little more than a month later, Diner-Denes brought him more news: "In Syrmia, says Diner, ten thousand Serbs have been killed as traitors; border areas have been depopulated [*entvolkerf*]." Redlich interpreted this as sign that a "systematic policy of extermination [*systematische Ausrottungspolitik*]" had been decreed against the Serbs.[7]

This kind of language prefigured Nazi terminology even though the Habsburg repression could scarcely compare in scale with the destruction unleashed in the same area by Hitler's Wehrmacht three decades later. Nevertheless, mass executions, concentration camps and deportation of the Serbian elite were all used by Franz Josef's military to ensure order in the occupied territories. In Anatolia, when war broke out, the Ottoman authorities deported thousands of Greeks away from the Asia Minor seaboard into the interior. Then, in 1915–1916, they killed perhaps as many as 1 million Armenians in an organized campaign of systematic massacre—executing some, leaving others to starve to death on forced marches. "Who now remembers the Armenians?"—Hitler's famous question of 1939—referred back to these events, as did Franz Werfel's thinly disguised anti-Nazi allegory of the 1930s, *The Forty Days of Musa Dagh.*

There were other, less extreme, ways of dealing with the issue of minorities. One policy with a future was what the experts benignly called "population transfer." Perhaps the most dramatic instance of this—the moment which marked the definitive end of the old Ottoman world—was the compulsory bilateral exchange of populations agreed between Greece and

Turkey in 1923: more than 1 million Greek Orthodox former Ottoman citizens were moved to Greece from Asia Minor, while 380,000 Muslims left Greece for Turkey. In fact, the total number of refugees involved was probably closer to 2 million, when one takes into account the other Greek refugees from the Black Sea littoral and eastern Thrace, as well as the many Muslims who had fled from elsewhere in the Balkans. Exception was made only for the Greek community in Constantinople, and for Muslims in western Thrace. A huge proportion of the inhabitants of both countries—at least one fifth in the Greek case—had thus experienced exile, flight and deprivation, while the state itself had to tackle problems of relief, sanitation, resettlement and the economic dislocation that came from uprooting communities in such numbers. But from the nationalist perspective, which Kemal Atatürk and Eleuthérios Venizélos—the two countries' dominant figures—shared, the population exchange was vitally important in helping to create ethnically homogeneous nation-states: the Greek province of Macedonia became overwhelmingly Greek (89 percent in 1923 compared with 43 percent in 1912), while the Turkish Anatolian coast became almost entirely Muslim, and Izmir— formerly known as the "infidel" because of its predominantly Christian population—rose from the ashes as a Turkish port.

Although the Greco-Turkish population exchange always appealed to international power brokers as a rational means of improving peace—and indeed did help improve relations between the two states after 1930—it was not followed up during the interwar period. Instead the Balkan states were made to sign minority-rights treaties by the Great Powers, which were monitored by the League of Nations. These treaties went beyond the old nineteenth-century protection of individuals to cover collective rights, whose importance the results of the war had underlined. In 1918, Romania had acquired not only huge new territories but also substantial

Hungarian, German, Ukrainian and Jewish populations. Only 72 percent of the population were ethnic Romanians. Nearly 15 percent of the population of the Kingdom of the Serbs, Croats and Slovenes did not belong to one of these three groups. One fifth of the population of Bulgaria was not Bulgarian. Greece—wrestling with more than 1 million refugees in a total population of just over 6 million—had Slavs, Jews and Muslim minorities. Even Albania, with its small Greek minority, was incorporated in the new minority-rights regime.[8]

The new system, however, satisfied neither minority nor majority. The former found that their complaints fell on deaf ears, since it turned out that there was no effective enforcement machinery at the league's disposal. The latter were irritated by an arrangement that allowed other states to intervene in their internal affairs. Grappling with enormous problems of reconstruction and development in a period of economic crisis and political uncertainty, Balkan states could not help resenting any action that reminded them of their own weakness. When we read of the uphill task the league faced in obliging the Albanian government in the 1930s to permit the Greek minority its own schools, it is easier to grasp how far the minority-rights regime had fallen short of expectations.[9]

Balkan states were in effect free to treat their minorities much as they wished. Rapid territorial expansion meant they often imposed their authority in the manner of colonial powers, sending gendarmes, teachers, settler farmers and tax collectors into remote provinces among peoples who spoke different languages. The Greeks in their "new lands," the Romanians in Bessarabia and Bukovina, the Serbs in their "new southern regions" and indeed in Croatia, Bosnia and Montenegro too, all saw themselves building a new state amid basically unfriendly populations. None went to quite the lengths of the interwar Polish state, which, in its struggle with Ukrainian nationalists, ended up burning villages and sending in the army; but there was systematic repression all the same. Minorities were frequently discriminated against in property disputes and forced to speak the new language of the state in public; their own remained for behind closed doors. "All the Macedonians have had to Serbianize their names by ending them with 'itch' instead of 'off,' " wrote Henri Pozzi in 1935; in Greece surnames ended in "os" or "is."[10]

As their new rulers suspected, many among these minorities did harbor revisionist sentiments: having seen how quickly and dramatically borders had changed between 1912 and 1922, they hoped to change them again. Croat and Macedonian émigré organizations plotted to overthrow the Versailles settlement, aligning themselves with revisionist powers like Fascist Italy. Macedonian autonomists virtually ran parts of western Bulgaria as a separate fiefdom and destabilized Bulgarian politics until the army stepped in. Hungarian and especially German minorities were regarded as potential fifth columns—a suspicion justified so far as the Germans were concerned by the Nazi use of ethnic Germans abroad for foreign policy goals. When the Second World War broke out, the revisionist agenda was traced on the map of southeastern Europe: Yugoslavia disappeared again and Albania, Bulgaria and Hungary expanded at the expense of Romania and Greece.

However, ethnic repression was not the whole story and should not be viewed in isolation from the broader governing philosophy of twentieth-century Balkan elites. It was liberals rather than conservatives who tended to advocate the least tolerant policies toward minorities. They did so because they saw themselves as embarked on a policy of state modernization in which a strong central power would drag their country into the twentieth century through active social and economic reforms. By almost all indicators (for instance, literacy rates, crop yields or longevity), the Balkans lagged behind the rest of Europe: the modernizers' task was immense. They were against the cultural fragmentation produced by allowing minorities their own schools and in favor of building more state schools so that they would learn the majority language. But it was not just minorities they suspected; they targeted all groups that might slip beyond their control, whether these were the communal self-governing structures of ethnic minorities, the Church, brigands, or potentially rebellious workers' or peasants' movements. They were also, at least in the 1920s, in favor of industrialization, the reform of agriculture and access to financial markets abroad—policies that required the participation of peoples with urban skills and languages, such as Germans, Jews and other minority groups. Liberal state-building, in other words, was unsympathetic to minority aspirations, but it was not entirely exclusionary. Repression was often not so much the ultimate goal as an aspect of the modernization of the state.

There was a sharp contrast here with the Nazi policy of defining and treating minorities in accordance with the principles of biological racism; this found only a faint echo in the Balkans. By learning the language and perhaps modifying one's name, assimilation was possible for Greeks in Albania, Vlachs and Slavs in Greece, Ukrainians and Macedonians in Romania; it was possible for religious outsiders like Jews and Muslims if they converted. Only in Romania did anti-Semitic governments condone pogroms and boycotts and limit Jewish enrollment in the universities. Extremist anti-Semitic movements such as the National Christian Party and the fascistic Iron Guard attracted considerable support there. In late 1940, after the Iron Guard finally entered the government, this violence erupted in a series of massacres, which killed thousands. But elsewhere, interwar anti-Semitism remained an element of popular Christian culture with little political impact. And in general, Balkan states did not bother with defining minorities in law, still less with forbidding interaction on racial grounds or arranging for their segregation, expropriation or expulsion, as the Nazis would after 1933. Such measures presupposed a degree of faith in science and bureaucracy that was absent in the impoverished, poorly administered, rural societies of southeastern Europe.[11]

After 1941, however, Nazi occupation brought to the surface—indeed deliberately exploited—the tensions simmering between ethnic groups and offered some minorities the chance to turn the tables on their interwar masters. For the first time in the modern era, Croatia won independence, as a puppet state of the Axis; it was ruled by an extreme nationalist party, the Ustache, which had failed to win much support before the war. This government banned the use of the Cyrillic alphabet, persecuted Serbs and Jews, and set up a one-party state whose aim was "to work for the principle that the Croatian people alone will always rule in Croatia." Its legal definition of Croatian nationality was woolly ["one of Aryan origin who has proven by his conduct that he did not engage in activities against the liberation efforts of the Croatian people"] and allowed loopholes that less hard-line civil servants could apply with discretion. But there was nothing woolly about the violence the regime unleashed almost immediately, mostly against Serbs and Jews, under the eyes of a far from critical Catholic Church. This led to the imprisonment and death of several hundred thousand people, notably in the Jasenovac camp, and gave a huge boost to the emergence of the partisan resistance movement.[12]

The Nazi occupation triggered off ethnic civil war more widely in the Balkans. Serb Chetniks talked of their intention "to cleanse Bosnia of everything that is not Serb" and killed tens of thousands of non-Serbs. Bulgarian troops annexed parts of Greek Thrace, killed thousands of civilians, banned the use of Greek and tried to resettle the province with Bulgarians. A similar policy was attempted in former Yugoslav Macedonia, but in both cases wartime colonization was a failure. Partisan reprisals and the hardships of wartime outweighed the attractions of free land and property. Given that agrarian resettlement in borderlands was usually a limited success even in peacetime—from Yugoslav efforts in interwar Macedonia to Greek efforts on its northern border in the 1950s, peasants rarely stayed put and usually followed the general drift toward the safety and wealth offered by cities—it is not surprising that it failed during the war. What is significant is that it was tried, for it indicates that for some Balkan states (as indeed for Nazi Germany itself), this war was not just about military victory but about permanent demographic engineering in new territories.[13]

Nor did the ethnic civil war come to an end as soon as the Germans pulled out. Fighting in Kosovo between Albanians and the Yugoslav partisans lasted for months, even years in some areas. Ethnic Germans were expelled from Voivodina and Romania, and their lands resettled. Albanians were driven out of northwestern Greece in 1944–1945, and the Greek civil war, which lasted from 1946 to 1949, became in part a war between the Athens government and the members of the Slavic-speaking minority in the north, who hoped to win some form of autonomy and perhaps connection with the Communist states emerging over the border.[14]

By 1950, the ethnic composition of the Balkans had been drastically altered. Its Jewish population dropped from roughly 856,000 in 1930 to under 50,000. Hundreds of thousands of ethnic Germans were expelled from Yugoslavia and deported from Romania. Slavs and Albanians fled northern Greece and the Serbs fled Kosovo. As a result of total war, genocide and large movements of refugees throughout the first half of the twentieth century, ethnic homogeneity had increased in all the Balkan states. Nevertheless, substantial minorities remained—among them, Muslims in Bulgaria, Greece and Bosnia and Hungarians in Romania.

In Yugoslavia, Tito attempted to solve the country's deeply rooted national problems by substituting multinational rule by a single dictatorial party for the interwar system of rule by Serbs and the Karajordje dynasty. At one stage, he even sought to use the idea of Communist federation as a means of dominating Bulgaria, Albania and Greece. While this dream ended with the Yugoslav break with Moscow in the summer of 1948, federalism remained the Communist strategy for handling nationalities within Yugoslavia. "Brotherhood and unity" may not have been a reality but it was something more than a slogan. Even after the Tito–Stalin split, Moscow's hegemony in Eastern Europe helped to ensure that minority issues and irredentism, while never entirely absent, would not disrupt relations between states in the way they had before 1940. But the tensions had not vanished, and would reemerge when communism collapsed.[15]

———

In the first half of the twentieth century, land was worked by the majority of the inhabitants of the Balkans, coveted by diplomats and fought over by armies. Balkan states shared the hunger for land found throughout Europe, believing in the need to expand—whether to redeem unredeemed brethren, to regain provinces they claimed by historical right or simply to demonstrate the nation's vitality in a Darwinian world. In the decade after 1914, Greece's territory and population both increased by nearly a quarter; Romania grew from 53.5 to 122.3 thousand square miles and from 7.5 to 17.6 million people. Bulgaria, which had lost territory, dreamed of rebuilding the San Stefano giant state it had been briefly promised in 1878. Albania, whose borders were formally agreed upon only in the early 1920s, looked to its irredenta in Greece and Yugoslavia.

Yet the urgent issue facing all these states after a decade of war was how to make this land feed the people who lived on it. Before 1912, transatlantic emigration on an enormous scale had demonstrated the difficulty of this task: several millions of impoverished peasants fled southeastern Europe—from Slovenia to the Peloponnese—for the United States in despair at the impoverished living offered by farming. With the closing of the prewar emigration routes after 1921, the new states of southeastern Europe had to show they could function as viable economies.

War made everyone aware of the need to be able to guarantee self-sufficiency, but it also vastly complicated this task. Beyond the huge problems of immediate postwar relief—so large that agencies such as the Near East Foundation, the League of Nations and the Rockefeller Foundation had to be called in to help—lay deeper structural dilemmas. The cost of prosecuting war had led by 1918 to the total economic and financial disruption of prewar monetary systems. Hence a priority for postwar states—before they could hope to raise loans on money markets abroad—was currency stabilization and banking reform. But this implied tightening taxes and reducing spending.

In one respect, peasants benefited enormously at the war's end: fear of Bolshevism spreading from Russia to eastern Europe made governments enact sweeping land reforms. By creating a class of peasant smallholders, politicians hoped to buy social tranquillity and prevent revolution. Hence peasant smallholdings increased their already dominant presence in the Balkans at the expense of large landholders. But the political benefits of this move were offset by the economic costs: parceling out the land forced farmers into cash crop production, increased their dependency on market forces and pushed them into debt. By the early 1930s, peasant indebtedness was a millstone around the neck of agrarian reformers, and the modernization of the countryside looked as far off as ever. As crop prices plummeted on world markets, peasants' incomes fell, yet they continued to bear the bulk of the national tax burden, which in all Balkan countries was sharply weighted toward indirect taxes on consumption goods. "A state cannot be democratic," warned the preamble to the 1923 Romanian tax law, "if at the moment when the large rural property disappears, it allows a few people to accumulate fortunes from trade and industry while leaving the mass of the people in the state of serfs of yesterday."[16]

Why did peasants not take advantage of the democratic rights they enjoyed to vote pro-peasant parties into office? The fact that Balkan parliamentary systems were, behind the liberal façade, corrupt and autocratic systems that retained power in the hands of courts, cliques of military officers and urban elites was only part of the answer. The weakness of peasant politics was one of the striking features of interwar Europe. Who today remembers the Green International, which was formed to unite the peasant parties of Europe against both Red Communists and White reactionaries? In theory, a largely peasant society should have seen parliamentary governments responsive to agrarian needs, but in reality peasants—still mostly illiterate, slow to move, reluctant to travel—were hard to mobilize politically. Peasant parties did emerge in Bulgaria and Romania, but they were neutralized—by force in the case of the Bulgarian Agrarian Union, which won a sweeping electoral victory before being ousted in a coup. The Romanian National Peasant Party held power for two years until its leader, Iuliu Maniu, resigned in a dispute with the King. The popular Croatian Peasant Party was marginalized for most of the interwar era by a Serb-dominated political elite. In Greece, agrarian parties remained largely irrelevant to a system polarized between royalists and republicans.[17]

More fundamentally, these parties had no real answer to the economic problems their countries faced. Lightening peasant tax loads and encouraging the spread of credit cooperatives would not solve the structural crisis of overpopulation and underindustrialization that confronted Balkan states. Smallholders could not compete on world markets; but they could not retreat back into the nineteenth century and self-sufficiency either, since they had debts to pay and rapidly growing families to feed. Despite the idealization of the peasant life promoted by urban intellectuals and new official tourist offices, it was evident that the solution to growth and prosperity did not lie in the villages. Peasants streamed into the cities in the 1920s and 1930s, but there were not enough jobs there either.

In the brief moment of optimism in the 1920s, between the end of postwar reconstruction and the Wall Street crash, most states in the Balkans opted to rebuild by rejoining the liberal international economy. They established independent central banks, joined the gold standard and tried to attract foreign investors by keeping budgets tight and repaying their debts. French, British and American funds poured into the region. However, international capitalism was a hard taskmaster. After 1930, Balkan exports dried up and a debt crisis loomed. Neither the British nor the French governments would allow Balkan states to earn foreign exchange by taking specified quantities of their goods. The result, by 1932, was widespread debt default, suspension of exchange rates and the collapse of the open international economic order that had been so deliberately rebuilt after 1918.

Thus in the 1930s, Balkan economies were thrown back upon their own resources. Raising tariff barriers and rationing foreign exchange, the state was forced to adopt a more directive and interventionist stance: for the first time, governments attempted to plan the allocation of resources, to protect their farmers by buying up the harvest and writing off their debt. Industrial growth in the 1930s was buoyant for a few years, while barter trade with the Third Reich substituted for the collapse of former markets. On the other hand, attempts to coordinate trade policy regionally through regular Balkan conferences met with very limited success and the efforts of some politicians to move toward a Balkan Federation made little headway.[18]

The economic crisis also eroded the frail foundations of parliamentary government. Even before 1930, interwar democratic institutions had failed to win legitimacy. Greece was plagued by incessant military coups and conspiracies. The dispute over the 1921 constitution in Yugoslavia exposed the gulf dividing the main Serbian and Croatian parties, a gulf that yawned inescapably following the assassination of the Croatian Peasant Party leader Stjepan Radić on the floor of the parliament. In Bulgaria, the Agrarian Prime Minister Aleksandŭr Stamboliskii was brutally assassinated after a coup. In Albania, Ahmed Bey Zogu established permanent rule by invading the country with a mercenary force in 1924 and having himself declared first president and then king. Communist parties, which briefly threatened in the early 1920s to gain widespread support, were banned in most countries. The main threat to liberal democracy between the wars came rather from the right.

After 1929, right-wing dictatorship replaced democracy everywhere in the Balkans. But the form of dictatorship was not fascism—rule by a mass party, coming to power through the democratic process—but authoritarian government by kings and their handpicked ministers. Nothing so revealed the weakness of mass politics in southeastern Europe as the fact that both left-wing and even popular fascist movements, like the Romanian Iron Guard, were so easily crushed and suppressed by the state. King Alexander dissolved parliament in the Kingdom of the Serbs, Croats and Slovenes in 1929, and henceforth ruled the country, now hopefully renamed Yugoslavia, through a personal dictatorship. In Bulgaria, King Boris followed suit in 1935, turning the assembly into a consultative body, and holding elections under close police supervision. King George of Greece dispensed with parliament in 1936; the much disliked Carol II of Romania had the popular fascist leader Corneliu Codreanu arrested and shot, created his own new Party of the Nation which struck observers as "a complete flop," and presided over a Government of National Union.[19]

Thus, despite the region's early experience of democratic politics, mass parties of the left and right failed to survive. By the end of the 1930s, the parliamentary system and political parties had disappointed the hopes invested in them by liberal intellectuals. Few mourned their passing. Yet the royal dictators and their henchmen were themselves uncertain of their mission and little loved; they were too obviously defenders of the prevailing order, too unprepared for the radical socioeconomic changes that were necessary to bring Balkan states out of the dead end of agrarian underemployment. This disillusionment both with bourgeois politicians and with the conservatives who had succeeded them paved the way for the emergence after 1945 of leftist projects of economic renewal under the eyes of the Soviet Union.

———

In the 1940s, the devastating shock of total war and its aftermath swept away the prewar political elites. Nazi (and then Soviet) occupation underlined in the starkest way the inability of the state to protect its citizens from violence, malnutrition and impoverishment. Greece suffered a devastating famine after the state failed to gain control of the country's food supply; Yugoslavia was dismembered and subjected to a regime of reprisals against civilians, internal civil war and social dislocation that left hundreds of thousands dead. The flight into exile of the Greek and Yugoslav heads of state estranged them from their own subjects. By 1943–1944, mass resistance movements, dominated by Communists, seemed poised to take over power once the Germans withdrew.

In October 1944, Churchill and Stalin agreed on postwar spheres of influence in southeastern Europe: Greece would fall under the British and the Americans; the rest would be left to the Soviet Union. The Greek Communists, however, refused to believe there had been a carve-up and were defeated only after a long civil war, which, by the time it ended in 1949, left more people dead, imprisoned or uprooted than German occupation itself had done. Thus the crisis of the Greek state lasted the entire decade of the 1940s and was resolved only thanks to massive British and American military and financial backing for anti-Communist forces. In Yugoslavia and Albania, on the other hand, Communist partisans quickly seized power. The Red Army passed through Yugoslavia in pursuit of the withdrawing Germans, but Tito's takeover was a domestic affair, achieved entirely through the military predominance of his partisan movement. Rivals like the Serbian Chetniks, the Croatian Ustache and Slovenian collaborationist units were crushed within a year.

In Bulgaria and Romania, the war itself touched society less than did its aftermath. Both countries were aligned with the Axis, which allowed them to escape the harrowing experiences of their neighbors, but meant that Germany's defeat brought about the collapse and discrediting of the old ruling elites. They suffered their own occupation by Soviet troops, who requisitioned grain from the peasants far more thoroughly than the Germans had and helped create a Communist movement capable of taking and retaining power. In

Bulgaria, in particular, there was a violent purge of the old state administration in which wartime collaborators as well as potential enemies from the old prewar political class were killed, imprisoned or exiled; in Romania, the government also settled scores with old ethnic enemies, notably the Germans. Both saw Communist Party memberships rise sharply from a tiny base—14,000 to 422,000 in Bulgaria, for instance, between September 1944 and 1946—for in these countries the form of party expansion that had come about elsewhere through wartime resistance to Nazi occupation had, for obvious reasons, not taken place.

By 1950, the fighting was over and the Balkans turned into a laboratory for the competition between the Free World and Soviet communism to lead traditional agrarian societies toward modernity. All the Balkan states had to industrialize to create jobs for their rapidly growing populations; all, in the longer term, needed to catch up with the standard of living in the rest of Europe. The contrast between the two sides of the Iron Curtain fascinated contemporary observers. "Will the ordinary man or woman, not as a political or economic animal, but as a human being, find life more worth living on the Eastern or the Western side of the border?" asked Elisabeth Barker, an experienced British observer in 1948. Barker herself noted the contrast between the anarchy of policy in Greece and rigid control to the north, between "a sure if hard minimum of social security at the price of a big sacrifice in human freedom, and social insecurity which puts the individual at the mercy of social parasites."[20]

Many Western intellectuals felt the Communists had the right economic strategy for the region. They did not necessarily admire the roughness of Communist methods, but they were inclined to see the policies themselves as not only a vast improvement on interwar stagnation, but likely to lead to permanent structural changes in the Balkan economy. "These far-reaching plans strike the imagination," wrote the historian Hugh Seton-Watson in 1954. "Even a foreign observer cannot fail to be affected by the enthusiasm and optimism of the planners. Moreover it is certain that large-scale industrialization, public works and mechanization of agriculture are the right remedies for the rural overpopulation and poverty, and the lack of manufactured goods, which were so striking in the old Eastern Europe."[21]

"Greece more than any East European country," he went on, "needs a program of planned industrialization," and he warned that it would be reliant on foreign aid for years to come. Although the former never materialized, the forecast was accurate: after the announcement of the Truman Doctrine in 1947, Greece turned into the largest beneficiary per capita of American largesse in the world, receiving more than $3 billion in military and economic assistance by 1963. Thereafter, an association agreement with the Common Market gave the country privileged access to Western European markets. Considering the huge extent of foreign capital inflows, growth rates were high but not exceptional, based on exports of textiles, on the remittances of thousands of laborers in West Germany, and increasingly upon the rise of mass tourism—2 million visitors a year by 1974, 6 million by 1980. Inside the country, capital was invested less in industry than in real estate, consumption goods and the service sector. The Greek state played a huge role in the economy, building roads and improving communications but doing little to foster manufacturing or other industries.

Growth on the other side of the Iron Curtain was initially much higher than in Greece. Communist governments made forced investment in heavy industry the cornerstone of their economic policies. They controlled consumption and, with none of Greece's access to American aid, channeled domestic funds into capital goods. Following the Soviet model, but in a less extreme form, they tried to collectivize the farms—with limited success—and conscripted civilian labor in various forms. Their efforts to declare "class war in the countryside" encountered determined peasant resistance in the early 1950s. Nevertheless, rapid electrification, new machine-tool industries, as well as the extension of road and rail systems, all signaled the Communists' determination to succeed where their predecessors had failed, and to make Balkan nation-states economically viable and modern. In 1939, 24 percent of Bulgarian national income was from industry and 56 percent from agriculture; by 1952 these figures were 47 percent and 34 percent. In Romania 76 percent of the prewar labor force had worked the land, and only 11 percent were in industry; by 1986 these figures were 28 percent and 45 percent, respectively. Had the Communist states not been forced to trade with the USSR but with Western Europe, as Greece was, their growth would have been faster still.[22]

Within a couple of decades, the revolutionary scale of social transformation on both sides of the Iron Curtain was unmistakable. Growth rates were unprecedentedly high, and the stagnation of the interwar years seemed to have been left behind. In a single remarkable generation, peasant village societies had made the leap to modern urban life. "It is all changing—and changing fast," noted *The Balkans,* a 1966 Time-Life book.

> The old Balkans—that world of passionate, near-mystical nationalism and deeply felt clan loyalties—will not last out the century, not even in the remote mountain enclaves of Albania and Montenegro. Like some hungry plant, Western technology puts down its tendrils everywhere. Tireless work brigades dynamite the mountain passes.... Tractors and disc harrows churn up the collective fields.... The shepherds are driven each morning to the pastures in trucks. On the Black Sea coast, the state tourist trusts build glass and pre-stressed concrete resort hotels.

The historian William McNeill, who visited Greece at intervals between 1947 and 1974, was even more forthright: "If satisfaction of human wants and aspirations is taken as the criterion," he wrote, "then the development of Greece across the last thirty years must be viewed as an extraordinary success story. Things that seemed impossible in 1945 have in fact come true for millions of individual Greeks."[23]

Cities expanded at an astonishing rate: between 1960 and 1991, Athens grew from 1.9 to 3 million, Bucharest from 1.4 to 2.2 million, Belgrade from 585,000 to 1.1 million: smaller cities such as Thessaloniki, Skopje and Sarajevo more than doubled the number of their inhabitants. High-rise apartment blocks encircled the old nineteenth-century town centers from Bucharest to Larissa; even in the countryside, small market towns turned into concrete jungles with steel and glass office blocks, as well as asphalt streets with growing traffic problems. The countryside began to empty and ghost villages emerged in the hills. By the 1980s, it was rare to find peasants wearing traditional costume outside the most remote and deprived areas. Peasants moved away from the countryside and brought up children who went to school, developed new conceptions of consumption and leisure and earned enough money to take vacations by the Black Sea, the Adriatic or the Aegean.

On the other hand, peasants retained their attachment to the village and soil even after moving into towns and changing their pattern of life. Religious sentiment was often stronger than Communist atheism; more important, perhaps, villages still supplied fresh food, pigs and fruit more reliably and cheaply than the officially rationed distribution and retail system. Social networks were transplanted from the village or family into government, the army and the economy. In other words, urbanization often meant the village being brought into the city. And perhaps in some ways taking it over too: the personalized interactions, gifts and favors which lubricated dealings with state officialdom could be misinterpreted by the unaware as forms of "corruption" rather than a natural response to the impersonal mechanisms of modern government.

In some respects, the contrast between communism and capitalism turned out to matter less than might have been thought. Patterns of growth were different but overall rates of growth were similar. Income inequality was greater in Greece than in Communist states, but then average incomes were also higher. On both sides of the Iron Curtain, income gaps widened between rural and urban workers. Across the Balkans, the social institutions of the modern welfare state were put in place—mass schooling and university education, hospitals and agricultural cooperatives. There were 26,500 students in higher education in prewar Romania, 157,000 by 1957. Across the region, meanwhile, the rural economy was replaced by the city, illiteracy disappeared, new roads eradicated peasant isolation, and villages ceased to reproduce themselves.

There were, needless to say, substantial political differences. Only in Nicolae Ceausescu's police state in Romania was the shift to urban life taken to the extreme of the deliberate destruction of peasant life and the creation of new "systematized" concrete agro-towns. Between the systematic surveillance of leftists in post-civil-war Greece and the spread of the secret police in Romania was a difference of kind, not degree—even if the former had more corrosive effects upon the country's life than many outsiders realized. The conformist anticommunism of Greek officialdom limited intellectual and cultural freedom but not to the extent of Marxist-Leninism to the north.[24]

Much discussion behind the Iron Curtain centered around the possibilities of effecting economic reform within a one-party state. In Yugoslavia, Communist reformists tried to reconcile centralized planning with the law of supply and demand in order, in their words, to create "a modern, highly productive, stable and rational market economy." But this was like trying to square the circle. Prices rose sharply, as did unemployment, and growth rates dropped. Private enterprise was permitted only on a limited scale and the lack of management experience with competitive business hindered all efforts to modernize and streamline state firms. Worker discontent was more serious under communism than capitalism: workers responded to economic decentralization and the relaxation of controls in Yugoslavia in particular with resentment at Party fat cats and a surge of nationalism. In Bulgaria and Romania, in contrast, there was less reform and greater police repression prevented overt opposition.[25]

From the mid-1970s onward, the contrast between capitalist Greece and the socialist north became much more marked. Oil shocks and a slowdown in the global economy forced change everywhere. But Communist regimes, which had devoted such energy to building up heavy industry in a bid for national self-sufficiency, found now that having successfully answered the economic problems of the 1930s, the questions had changed. In the late twentieth century, heavy, labor-intensive industry protected by a national state was unable to compete with capitalist rivals overseas. Not even heavy borrowing from Western banks—the replay in the 1980s under communism of a strategy pursued sixty years earlier by their detested bourgeois predecessors—could save them. Only through extreme repression could growing foreign debt burdens be repaid. Using a secret police whose size and agent networks dwarfed the Gestapo, Ceausescu repaid Romania's creditors at the expense of the living standards of his own population. However, elsewhere—and especially in Yugoslavia—the central state was simply too weak to do this. The Bulgarian state was stronger than the Yugoslav, with experience in the concentration of resources that stretched back to before the war, and its resort to foreign borrowing was far less, in part due to generous Soviet assistance.[26]

In Greece, the chronic weakness of the state was offset by the flexibility of the private sector, by the savings of individuals with long experience in keeping their money out of the hands of the state, and by transfers of resources from the European Community, of which Greece had become a member—and a beneficiary—in 1981. But democracy—reintroduced after the fall of the colonels' junta (1967–1974)—also allowed space for popular dissatisfaction without threatening the political system as a whole. After 1974 Greece enjoyed a stable two-party democratic system, in which socialist and conservative parties alternated in power. In Communist states, by contrast, the economic crisis meant a challenge to the legitimacy of the political system itself.

The consequences would be gravest in Yugoslavia, where Tito's death in 1980 had already weakened the federation. The Party's slogan ("After Tito, Tito!") was a confession of ideological bankruptcy. The International Monetary Fund came to the government's aid but only temporarily: "stabilization" required hard political choices. Freezing wages alienated workers; Serbian and Slovene political elites in particular resisted the squeeze. Thus the economic crisis eroded the strength of the federal government and opened the way for nationalist struggles at the regional and republic level over economic resources and political power.

———

"Marxism cannot be reconciled with nationalism," Lenin had once claimed. "In place of all forms of nationalism, Marxism advances internationalism, the amalgamation of all nations in the higher unity." But in fact postwar Communist regimes soon found that, whether they liked it or not, they had to come to terms with the power of popular nationalism in the Balkans. Communist rule had not led to nation-states being subsumed within a broader federation, as some interwar theorists had hoped. The post-1918 order of states remained largely intact.[27]

Minorities had mostly shrunk. But in their behavior toward their minorities, Communist regimes looked rather similar to their predecessors in the way they combined repression and assimilation in the name of modernization. Romania veered in its treatment of the Transylvanian Hungarians from the apparent liberalism of the 1952 constitution, which had envisaged setting up a Hungarian autonomous region, to the forced assimilation policy pursued a few years later as the Party itself adopted a more nationalist tendency and came out against "manifestations of national isolationism."

Bulgarian campaigns against the country's Turkish minority forced thousands to flee abroad in 1950 and again in 1968. In the early 1970s many Muslim villagers were forced to hand in their old ID cards and to thank officials publicly for their new Bulgarian names. The 1984 assimilation campaign attacked fasting during Ramadan as a "destructive superstition." "The Bulgars of the Rhodope regions have shaken off their Islamic fundamentalism," commented Stanko Todorov in 1985, "liberated themselves from the influence of conservatism in their lives and strengthened their Bulgarian patriotic consciousness." Bulgaria was, according to him, a "one-nation state" in which "there are no parts of any other people and nation." In 1989, in its death throes, the Communist regime triggered off another mass exodus in which 300,000 Muslims left for Turkey. By 1990, however, Bulgarian troops were stemming the flow and nearly 130,000 returned. The same year, the new post-Communist government accepted the restoration of Muslims' former names and arrested Todor Zhivkov, the former head of state and

Party leader, accusing him among other things of "incitement of ethnic hostility and hatred."[28]

In Yugoslavia, in contrast, the collapse of communism had very different consequences and made the plight of minorities worse, not better. The two forces preserving the unity of the federal state were the power of the Communist Party and the person of Tito himself. Under Tito, tensions between the republics were settled at the federal level of the state and Party apparatus. Even before his death in 1980, strains had been apparent in both Belgrade and Zagreb as nationalist currents emerged among Party cadres. The Bosnian party, which had the most hard-line leadership of any of the republics, became increasingly important in supporting the federal leadership against the centrifugal tendencies operating from the grass roots. But after Tito's death, the federal leadership, weakened by the protracted economic crisis, was less successful in balancing the competing claims of the different nationalities. With the rise of Serbian nationalism in the mid-1980s, the system began to break down.

Tito's regime had been based upon a highly elaborate system of official national groups, and even created several "new" ones. As early as November 1943, Yugoslav Communists had recognized Macedonia as a separate republic within the federation and declared its inhabitants to be members of a separate, "Macedonian" nation. In 1971 Bosnian Muslims were recognized for the first time as a separate nation too. Yugoslavia was one of the last countries where the old Habsburg distinction between "nations" and "nationalities" was preserved: among the latter, the largest were the Albanians, settled mostly in the autonomous province of Kosovo. They increasingly outnumbered Serbs and other groups; Albanians were perhaps 85 percent of the total population of Kosovo and roughly 20 percent of the population of the neighboring republic of Macedonia.

Even before the collapse of communism, Slobodan Milosevic began to reassert Serb power in Kosovo and Voivodina. His policies were originally intended to bolster Serb influence within Yugoslavia. But as the federation's republics broke away it became clear that what Milosevic was fighting for was not Yugoslavia but rather the creation of a Greater Serbia that would allow Serb minorities in Croatia and Bosnia to remain part of the same overall political community as Serbs in Serbia and Montenegro. After 1991, international support for independent Croatia and Bosnia eventually caused even this policy to fail: Croatian Serbs were driven from the Krajina, and Bosnian Serbs were forced to give up territory and accept that they were part of Bosnia. At the decade's end, Milosevic suffered a further failure when NATO went to war with Serbia to carve out a separate self-governing territory for the Albanians in Kosovo. By 1999, the borders of the Republic of Serbia were almost back to where they had been in 1878 in the time of Milan Obrenović. Milosevic had failed; his sole success was that he retained power in Belgrade.

The use of mass expulsions to ensure permanent ethnic domination had been the goal of Serb policy in Bosnia after 1992; it was feared to be Serb policy in Kosovo too six years later. Historians read such policies back into Europe's past. Political scientists feared they might have a future. But whether the Yugoslav wars really indicated, as many foresaw, the emergence of a new "ethnic nationalism" could be doubted. It was easy, amid the gloom, to exaggerate. Potentially most destabilizing were the repercussions of the wars in Bosnia and Kosovo for neighboring areas. Tensions ran high between Serbia and Montenegro, though the latter's suspicion of Milosevic and dreams of real independence would always be tempered by uncertainty at what life would be like for a small Montenegrin state, flanked by Albania in the south, Croatia and Bosnia. More worrying still were the implications for stability in Albania and Macedonia if Kosovo eventually—as seemed highly likely—broke away from Serbia altogether. Irredentism seemed stronger among Albanians than most other peoples in southeastern Europe, perhaps because they had been deprived for so long of their freedom.

Elsewhere, though, the expansionism of the past seemed to have vanished. Only a few diaspora nationalists—in the United States, Australia or Canada—dreamed of fighting for a Greater Greece or San Stefano Bulgaria. Almost no one in the Balkans actually harbored such aspirations. Attitudes to land and territorial expansion had changed there as elsewhere in postwar Europe. Moreover, the shift from rural to urban societies had transformed the role of minorities and the authorities' attitude toward them. Moving from villages to towns meant leaving militarily sensitive border areas for more anonymous and less neuralgic political spaces. States in the Balkans either were in, or wished to join, European institutions that required their members to commit themselves to providing certain human and minority rights. And economic growth meant that countries which had formerly been exporters of labor now found that they were becoming importers instead: Greece was the first Balkan country to realize that new immigrant communities—from the Philippines, Pakistan, Ukraine—were turning it, willy-nilly, into a multicultural society.

As in the rest of Europe, then, the Balkans were seeing issues of nationalism and minority rights turning from a question of war and peace to one of border policing and urban coexistence. The long struggle to create a nation-state—of which the Yugoslav wars could be seen as the final phase—had taken the entire twentieth century. The irony was that just as this struggle ended, economic and political changes at the international level threw the very idea of the nation-state into question. The collapse of Communist one-party states signaled the most dramatic crisis of the old idea of socioeconomic transformation though the domestic policies of the individual state; but accession to the European Union in a more insidious and indirect way confronted Greece and future Balkan applicants with similar issues. In both cases, the dismantling of tariffs and protected state industries as well as the exposure to global competition meant the triumph of neoliberal forces. The traditional Balkan nation-state is no longer challenged by the old empires; it is not even challenged by the rivalry and hostility of neighbors; its main threat comes now from the international economy.

ON VIOLENCE

When I travelled in Europe, I saw everywhere things I did not particularly like. Fine—I did not say, "That is no good." I wanted to know why things were thus.

—OTTOMAN OFFICIAL IN CONVERSATION
WITH FRENCH PRIEST, 1848[1]

In the 1990s, the wars in the former Yugoslavia put the Balkans back on the map of Europe, and aroused anxious memories of the First World War. While the rest of the continent was coping with mass immigration, new regional diversities and what were often euphemistically termed "multicultural societies," southeastern Europe looked as if it was reverting to an earlier historical logic of territorial wars and ethnic homogenization. Was this Europe's past or its future?

Those who opposed Western intervention in the Balkans tended to blame Yugoslav President Milosevic less than long-run cultural determinants of behavior in the region. They saw ethnic diversity itself as a chronic source of tension in a part of the world that lay on the intersection of several major religions, and they interpreted ethnic cleansing not so much as part of the European logic of nation-state building but as the latest in a series of massacres and countermassacres that, according to them, constituted the stuff of Balkan history. "The conflict in Bosnia," British Prime Minister John Major stated in 1993, "was a product of impersonal and inevitable forces beyond anyone's control." The language was not new. A century earlier, Gabriel Hanotaux, the French foreign minister, had similarly termed anti-Armenian massacres in Anatolia as "one of those thousand incidents of struggle between Christians and Muslims."[2]

Yet for centuries, as this book has attempted to show, life in the Balkans was no more violent than elsewhere; indeed the Ottoman empire was better able than most to accommodate a variety of languages and religions. To Arnold Toynbee, witnessing its final days, it was evident that the source of conflict

lay outside the region. "The introduction of the Western formula [of the principle of nationalism] among these people,"
he wrote in 1922, "has resulted in massacre.... Such massacres are only the extreme form of a national struggle
between mutually indispensable neighbors, instigated by this
fatal Western idea." "Ethnic cleansing"—whether in the
Balkans in 1912–1913, in Anatolia in 1921–1922 or in erstwhile Yugoslavia in 1991–1995—was not, then, the sponta-
neous eruption of primeval hatreds but the deliberate use of
organized violence against civilians by paramilitary squads
and army units; it represented the extreme force required by
nationalists to break apart a society that was otherwise capable of ignoring the mundane fractures of class and ethnicity.[3]

To be sure, not everyone shares this view. In 1994 an Austrian reader of my book *Inside Hitler's Greece* suggested I had
been too harsh in my judgment of German military behavior
in the Balkans in the 1940s, given that—as recent events again
demonstrated, in his view—there was evidently a peculiar
propensity to violence among the people of the region. To
me, the wartime slave labor camp at Mauthausen indicated
that the Austrians did not have much to learn from the Bosnian Serbs about violence. But our argument was not really
about *violence* so much as about cruelty—behavior, not numbers. It was, after all, neither the peoples of the Balkans nor
their rulers who gave birth to the Gulag, the extermination
camp or the Terror. Wehrmacht soldiers (not to mention
other Nazi agencies) killed far more people in the Balkans
than were killed by them. What my correspondent objected
to was the manner in which the partisans had done their
killing.

During the Second World War, Nazi ideology too distinguished "necessary" impersonal violence from the cruel or
sadistic behavior of men who lost control of their feelings and
actions. In the trial of one officer, a Munich SS court in 1943

contrasted orderly and decent killing with the defendant's "cruel excesses," "sadism" and "vicious brutality." Such attitudes formed part of a longer Western effort to define rules of civilized warfare, which highlighted an ideal of individual self-control. Like others in that tradition, the Nazis saw primitive and oriental bloodthirstiness lingering in the Balkans.[4]

We can go back to Montaigne's essay on cruelty to see the new view emerging. Castigating men of his own times for their delight in suffering, he describes the grief he feels when unnecessary pain is inflicted upon humans and animals:

> I could hardly be persuaded before I had seene it, that the world could have afforded so marble-hearted and savage-minded men, that for the onely pleasure of murther would commit it; then cut, mangle and hacke other members in pieces; to rouze and sharpen their wits, to invent unused tortures and unheard-of torments.... As for me, I could never so much as endure, without remorse or griefe, to see a poore, sillie and innocent beast pursued and killed.[5]

The shift toward a "humanitarian" concept of pain and punishment—bound up with changing ideas of the human personality—was a very gradual one, stretching across the eighteenth and nineteenth centuries. Then relatively suddenly, between 1820 and 1860, the number of capital crimes was sharply reduced in Western Europe, older forms of punishment such as the rack, burning and decapitation were abandoned, while the modern prison evolved and replaced the public space as the main locus of state executions. "The spectacle, and even the very idea of pain," wrote John Stuart Mill in 1836, "is kept more and more out of sight by those classes who enjoy in their fulness the benefits of civilization." Thanks to "a perfection of mechanical arrangements impracticable in any but a high state of civilization," the infliction of pain can be handed over to "the judge, the soldier, the surgeon, the butcher and the executioner." And Mill continued: "It is in avoiding the presence not only of actual pain but of whatever suggests offensive or disagreeable ideas that a great part of refinement consists."[6]

A few years later, such sentiments animated a British traveler, Sir James Gardner Wilkinson, who tried to intervene in the border wars between the Ottoman rulers of Bosnia-Hercegovina and their Montenegrin neighbors. Upset by both sides' habit of decapitating enemies and displaying their heads in public, he wrote to the bishop-prince of Montenegro, the Vladika Petar, arguing that a custom "so shocking to humanity" actually prolonged hostilities by exciting the desire for revenge. He tried to explain "the difference between the sentiments engendered by a civilized war, and a war in which such a usage is adopted." It was only in 1820, we might note, that the heads of the Cato Street conspirators had been publicly displayed to the crowd in London.[7]

The reduction in public executions in mid-nineteenth-century Britain, Scandinavia and Germany reflected not just the emergence of new "civilized feelings" and new industrial equipment, but also the authorities' fears of disorderly crowds and their excitable passions. Rural peasant societies like those of southeastern Europe inhabited a different moral, mechanical and political universe. The Ottoman authorities were not worried about the riotous mob and they went in for exemplary public punishment; but for their part they regarded the European use of bodies for surgical experiment and dissection as sacrilegious and immoral. The Vladika Petar Njegos, who had recently felt obliged to avenge the Turkish killing of his own relatives in the usual fashion, courteously rejected Wilkinson's proposal as unworkable.[8]

"We may be poor but we have honor," an elderly Montenegrin woman told an interviewer recently, summing up the close relationship between peasant hardship and the code of honor. Western attitudes asserted the value of individual self-control; others were more concerned about preserving the family honor. Peasant communities had regulated life both officially and informally in terms of collective responsibility and sanctions since Byzantine times, if not earlier. Punishment, even by the state, long reflected the popular view that families were responsible for the misdeeds of their individual members. Peasants in nineteenth-century Serbia, for instance, proposed stamping out growing crime by exiling both the criminal and his family to special penal regions. Antibrigandage laws often deported or levied fines not only on the brigand but on his relatives too.[9]

Modernizing politicians were, however, drawn to the new norms of violence—individualized, private and impersonal rather than collective, familial and public. Building a modern state—in the Balkans as elsewhere—meant wresting violence, punishment and local lawmaking out of the hands of all unauthorized agents and centralizing them in the hands of civil servants. For them, in the words of a Greek journalist of the 1920s, the state had "a duty to show it stands above everyone and everything." Regular armies replaced self-armed groups; judicial and penal bureaucracies emerged in place of village courts and customary sanction; the brigands were hunted down. In Montenegro, where tribal law had been all-powerful, Vladika Petar II's successor, Prince Danilo Petrovic, imposed a new law code in 1851—less than a decade after Wilkinson's first intervention—and discouraged decapitation. He also outlawed the practice of blood feuding, which threatened to make it impossible to weld the country's tribes into a cohesive whole.[10]

The conquest of the new values was neither instantaneous nor complete. Wartime massacres unleashed by the Croatian Ustache against Jews and Serbs, especially at the Jasenovac death camp, or by the Romanian Iron Guard in their pogroms of 1940–1941 represented a fusion of older and newer mentalities and technologies. In 1947, during the Greek civil war, an outraged London *Daily Mirror* published a front-page photograph of armed royalists on horseback parading the heads of Greek rebels. "Heads Are Cheap" was the title of the article, which highlighted the "cruelties and atrocities" committed by regular police and army units. In fact, ministerial orders had previously been issued forbidding the display of decapitated heads and recommending the use of photographs instead to identify dead guerrillas. Behind the scenes, British officials deplored the use of the term "atrocity." They pointed out that "the exhibition of corpses of criminals was not confined to Greece and even in normal times was practiced in order to convince the frightened populace that a well-known murderer was dead." In poorly policed societies, decapitation proved the victim was dead and asserted the courage of his killer or the power of the state. Transporting entire bodies was burdensome and cameras were expensive—as American bounty hunters also knew. And far from heads being cheap, these ones were valuable, since prices had been fixed for them.[11]

Was there really, then, a special propensity to cruelty that lingered on in the Balkans into modern times? Perhaps it all depends on what one means by cruelty. One could, after all, tell a very different story. There were no Balkan analogues to the racial violence displayed by lynch mobs in the United States between 1880 and 1920 or to the class violence that labor protests elicited there and elsewhere. Western Europe had its own myths of revolutionary violence—from Sorel onward—whose impact was far greater there than in the continent's southeastern corner, yet these were commonly regarded as heroic rather than barbaric. Political violence between 1930 and 1960, from the Left and the Right, was no greater in the Balkans than elsewhere, whether we are comparing postwar Bulgarian and Soviet prisons, or Greek and Spanish camps after their respective civil wars.

Beyond politics, too, Balkan states have not been inclined to kill or incarcerate more of their citizens than other countries. Compared with the 11 million criminal suspects and 2 million prisoners in the United States and the huge prison population of Russia, contemporary southeastern Europe looks rather humane. In the United States 554 per 100,000 were behind bars in 1994; the corresponding rates were 195 in Romania, 63 in Macedonia and 16 in Greece. None of the Balkan prisoners faced the prospect of judicial execution, whereas the United States used the electric chair or lethal injection upon dozens of prisoners a year. And if it is hard to argue that Balkan states now are more cruel than others, it is equally hard to make the same charge of their societies: crime rates are not above European norms, least of all for violent crimes. Alcohol does not induce the number of assaults it does in Protestant Europe, nor does racial hatred.[12]

On the lookout for evidence of Balkan bloodthirstiness, however, Western observers have often mistaken the myths spun by nineteenth-century romantic nationalists for eternal truths. Across Europe, from Ireland to Poland, poetic visionaries dreamed of resurrection, sacrifice and blood spilled for the sake of the nation's future. To take but the best-known Balkan exemplar of this genre, *The Mountain Wreath*'s glorification of the supposed extermination of Muslims in Montenegro a century and a half earlier was the product of the Vladika Petar Njegos's poetic imagination, not of historical fact: it lauded as heroic atrocity the much less bloody real story of the gradual departure of Muslims from Montenegrin land over more than a century. The rise of the Kosovo legend during the twentieth century was similarly misleading—an indication of modern not medieval prejudices. In both cases, the emergence of Balkan epics of bloodshed and national unity was not fortuitous; they emerged at points in the nine-teenth century when the nation-building process was coming under particular strain. This, not the primeval past, was the origin of their ethnically polarized sentiments.[13]

Moreover, as was evident first in the Gulf War, the West has increasingly come to see war itself as a spectacle. NATO's intervention in Kosovo and Serbia utilized an impersonal and distant technology in order to reassure a Western public that a military campaign could now be waged with a minimum of casualties or bloodshed on either side. In this way, perhaps, war itself is being depersonalized, much as social violence had been earlier. Writing off Balkan violence as primeval and unmodern has become one way for the West to keep the desired distance from it. Yet, in fact, ethnic cleansing is not a specifically Balkan phenomenon. It took place through much of central and eastern Europe during and immediately after Hitler's war: more than fifty forced population movements took place in the 1940s, involving the death and transplanta-tion of millions of Germans, Poles, Ukrainians and many others. The roots of the ferocity of this latest cleansing lie not in Balkan mentalities but in the nature of a civil war waged with the technological resources of the modern era. Unlike national wars, civil wars do not unify society (in the way, for instance, the Second World War helped unify British society). On the contrary, they exacerbate latent tensions and differ-ences, and are fought out amid a total breakdown of social and governmental institutions.[14]

How might the Balkans look if the sign of violence was lifted for a moment? It is true that serious threats to peace still exist in southeastern Europe, perhaps more serious than else-where: Turkish–Greek relations, embittered in particular by Cyprus, will take more than an earthquake to improve, while NATO bombing of Kosovo has solved one problem (Serbian persecution of the Kosovar Albanians) only to create others

(Albanian persecution of Serbs, as well as the new relationship between Albania, Macedonia, Serbia and Kosovo itself). Just as the nation-building process is more recent and compressed in the Balkans, so ethnic nationalism remains stronger and civic traditions more fragile than elsewhere. Nevertheless, while Yugoslavia in the 1990s descended into war for its own reasons, other countries in the region have followed a more peaceful path. Occasional Greek references to "Northern Epirus" (i.e., southern Albania), Bulgarian dreams of "Macedonia," Romanian nostalgia for Bessarabia and Moldova are today faint and meaningless echoes of issues that provoked wars and invasions a century ago: politics there has ceased to gravitate around expansionism and national glory. Only perhaps some Albanian nationalists have yet to abandon the dreams given up by their neighbors.

During the Cold War, a social and economic revolution transformed the Balkans. The all-important shift to an urban, industrial—and now postindustrial—society brought fundamental changes to the nature of daily life and new challenges to domestic political elites. The ending of the Cold War has allowed the Balkans to participate in a different Europe, whose values are inscribed in its dominant cross-national institutions: the European Union, NATO and the CSCE (now the OSCE), for example. And it has transformed them geopolitically too, since they now find themselves at the center of a greatly expanded market that takes in the Black Sea, the former Soviet Union and central Asia, offering possibilities for business across a vaster area than at any time since the collapse of the Ottoman empire. In other words, the problems and perspectives for southeastern Europe today are not those of the past, but dilemmas familiar in one form or another to most European countries: how to reconcile older patterns of welfare provision with the competitive pressures of global capitalism; how to provide affordable energy while safeguarding the natural environment from pollution; how to prevent the total decline of rural ways of life, and to build the prosperous economies that alone will reduce the attractions of organized crime and allow democracy to flourish. Perhaps understanding the region's history can still clear the ground for an appreciation of the possibilities that lie ahead.

NOTES

INTRODUCTION: NAMES

1. Friedrich Nietzsche, *The Gay Science,* cited in M. Todorova, *Imagining the Balkans* (New York, 1997), p. 19.

2. Warrington W. Smyth, *A Year with the Turks* (New York, 1854), p. 169.

3. Earl of Albemarle [George Keppel], *Narrative of a Journey Across the Balcan* (London, 1831); M. von Tietz, *St. Petersburgh, Constantinople and Napoli di Romania in 1833 and 1834* (New York, 1836), p. 91; Lt.-Gen. A. Jochmus, "Notes on a Journey into the Balkan, or Mount Haemus in 1847," *Journal of the Royal Geographical Society* 24 (1854), pp. 36–86; E. Ollier, *Cassell's Illustrated History of the Russo-Turkish War* (London, n.d.), vol. 2, p. 15.

4. P. Vidal de la Blache and L. Gallois, *Geographie Universelle* (Paris, 1934), vol. 7, no. 2, pp. 395–96; J. Pinkerton, *Modern Geography: A Description of the Empires, Kingdoms, States and Colonies, with the Oceans, Seas and Isles in All Parts of the World* (London, 1802), vol. 1, p. 461; Jochmus, "Notes," p. 64. The earliest indigenous account is probably D. Filippides and G. Konstantas's 1791 *Geografia neoteriki;* see the edition edited by A. Koumarianou (Athens, 1988).

5. Rhigas in R. Clogg, ed., *The Movement for Greek Independence, 1770–1821* (London, 1976), pp. 157–63. E. A. Freeman, "Race and Language," *Contemporary Review* 29 (1877), pp. 711–41.

6. Cf. Ami Boué, *Recueil d'itineraires dans la Turquie d'Europe* (Vienna, 1854), vol. 2, pp. 327–32; H. F. Tozer, *Researches in the Highlands of Turkey* (London, 1869), vol. 1, pp. 393–97; Saint-Marc Girardin cited in T. G. Djuvara, *Cent projets de partage de la Turquie (1281–1913)* (Paris, 1914), p. 496.

7. F. Crousse, *La Péninsule greco-slave* (Brussels, 1876); T. Fischer, *Mittelmeerbilder* (Leipzig, 1906), p. 44; D. M. Brancoff (Dimitur Mishev), *La Macedoine et sa population chretienne* (Paris, 1905), p. 3; J. R. Mar-

riott, *The Eastern Question: An Historical Study in European Diplomacy* (Oxford, 1917), p. 21.

8. H. de Windt, *Through Savage Europe* (London, 1907), p. 15; Todorova, *Imagining the Balkans*, p. 122.

9. R. West, *Black Lamb and Grey Falcon* (London, 1943), vol. 1, p. 23.

10. E. Christiansen, *The Northern Crusades* (London, 1997), p. 2; on the two phases of Muslim Holy War against Europe, see B. Lewis, *The Muslim Discovery of Europe* (New York, 1982), pp. 20–28; K. M. Setton, *Prophecies of Turkish Doom* (Philadelphia, 1992), p. 4.

11. Setton, *Prophecies of Turkish Doom*, and K. M. Setton, *Europe and the Levant in the Middle Ages and the Renaissance* (London, 1974); Knolles cited in Lewis, *The Muslim Discovery of Europe*, p. 32; on Muslim and Turk as synonyms, see N. Matar, *Islam in Britain, 1558–1685* (Cambridge, 1998), p. 21.

12. L. Valensi, *Venezia e la Sublima Porta: La nascita del despota* (Bologna, 1989), pp. 41, 44; L. Stavrianos, *The Balkans since 1453* (New York, 1965), pp. 74–75.

13. Matar, *Islam in Britain*, pp. 14, 22.

14. See A. Pippidi, "La Decadence de l'Empire ottoman comme concept historique, de la Renaissance aux lumières," *Revue des Etudes Sud-Est Européennes* 35, no. 1–2 (1997), pp. 5–19.

15. As Pippidi notes, there was also a countercurrent, rather weaker, of pro-Turkish critics of contemporary European society, of whom Montesquieu was among the most prominent. Ibid., pp. 18–19.

16. A. J. Evans, *Through Bosnia and the Hercegovina on Foot* (London, 1877), p. 89; H. Holland, *Travels in the Ionian Islands, Albania, Thessaly, Macedonia etc. during the Years 1812 and 1813* (London, 1815), pp. 69–70; *The War Correspondence of Leon Trotsky: The Balkan Wars, 1912–1913* (New York, 1981), pp. 58–59.

17. E. A. Freeman, *Ottoman Power in Europe* (London, 1877), p. 1; A. Oakes and R. B. Mowat, eds., *The Great European Treaties of the Nineteenth Century* (Oxford, 1918), p. 177; see N. Sousa, *The Capitulatory Regime of Turkey: Its History, Origins, and Nature* (Baltimore, 1933), p. 162. See also J. C. Hurewitz, "Ottoman Diplomacy and the European State System," *Middle East Journal* 15 (1961), pp. 141–52.

18. Anon. (Lord JR), *The Establishment of the Turkish Empire* (London, 1828), p. 27; R. G. Latham, *The Ethnology of Europe* (London, 1852), p. 6; R. G. Latham, *The Nationalities of Europe* (London, 1863), vol. 2, p.

69; E. Joy Morris, *Notes of a Tour through Turkey, Greece, Egypt, Arabia Petraea to the Holy Land* (Philadelphia, 1842), vol. 1, p. 48; E. Durham, *The Burden of the Balkans* (London, 1905), p. 104.

19. Boué, *Recueil d'itineraires,* vol. 2, p. 331; on the expulsion of Muslims from Balkan states, see A. Toumarkine, *Les Migrations des populations musulmanes balkaniques en Anatolie (1876–1913)* (Istanbul, 1995), a useful source to set against the less balanced J. McCarthy, *Death and Exile: The Ethnic Cleansing of Ottoman Muslims, 1821–1922* (Princeton, N.J., 1995); on shrinking of Turkish usage, see B. Lory, "Parler le turc dans les Balkans ottomans au XIXe siècle," in F. Georgeon and P. Dumont, eds., *Vivre dans l'Empire ottoman* (Paris, 1997), pp. 237–45; on destruction of monuments, see M. Kiel, *Studies on the Ottoman Architecture of the Balkans* (Aldershot, Eng., 1990).

20. F. Moore, "The Changing Map of the Balkans," *The National Geographic Magazine* (February 1913), pp. 199–226.

21. J. V. de la Roiere, *Voyage en Orient* (Paris, 1836), p. 23; *War Correspondence of Trotsky,* p. 272.

22. Marriott, *Eastern Question,* p. 3; O. Halecki, *The Limits and Divisions of European History* (New York, 1962), pp. 47, 77–78.

23. T. Zhivkov cited in M. Kiel, *Art and Society of Bulgaria in the Turkish Period* (Maastricht, 1985), p. 34, n. 1.

24. My thanks to Dimitri Livanios for his very helpful formulations of these issues.

1. THE LAND AND ITS INHABITANTS

1. F. Braudel, *The Mediterranean* (London, 1972), vol. 1, pp. 25–53.

2. M. Newbigin, *The Mediterranean Lands* (London, 1924), p. 46; M. Adelaide Walker, *Through Macedonia to the Albanian Lakes* (London, 1864), p. 87.

3. A. J. Evans, *Through Bosnia and the Herzegovina on Foot* (London, 1877), p. 359; M. Djilas, *Land without Justice: An Autobiography of His Youth* (New York, 1958), p. 79.

4. A. Kinglake, *Eothen* (Oxford, 1982), p. 22.

5. M. von Tietz, *St. Petersburgh, Constantinople and Napoli di Romania in 1833 and 1834* (New York, 1836), p. 96.

6. H. F. Tozer, *Researches in the Highlands of Turkey* (London, 1869), vol. 1, p. 382.

7. T. Stoianovich, *Balkan Worlds: The First and Last Europe* (New York, 1994), p. 107.

8. M. Zdraveva, "The Menzil Service in Macedonia, Particularly around Bitolj, in the Period of Turkish Domination," *Etudes Balkaniques* 2 (1995), pp. 82–88; J. A. Blanqui, *Voyage en Bulgarie pendant l'année 1844* (Paris, 1845), pp. 102–3; Kinneir cited by Tozer, *Researches,* vol. 1, p. 150; Walker, *Through Macedonia,* p. 131; D. Warriner, ed., *Contrasts in Emerging Societies: Readings in the Social and Economic History of South-Eastern Europe in the Nineteenth Century* (London, 1965), p. 242; J. Baker, *Turkey* (New York, 1877), p. 389; the best study is B. Gounaris, *Steam over Macedonia, 1870–1912: Socio-Economic Change and the Railway Factor* (Boulder, Colo., 1993), esp. pp. 71–74.

9. J. C. Wagner, *Delineatio provinciarum pannoniae et imperii turcici in Oriente* (Augsburg, 1684), pp. 119–20; R. Halsband, ed., *The Complete Letters of Lady Mary Wortley Montagu,* vol. 1, *1708–1720* (Oxford, 1965), p. 340; K. Mihailovic, *Memoirs of a Janissary,* trans. B. Stulz (Ann Arbor, Mich., 1975), p. 163; E. S. Forster, ed., *The Turkish Letters of Ogier Ghiselin de Busbecq* (Oxford, 1927), p. 108.

10. Tietz, *St. Petersburgh;* J. K. Vasdravellis, *Klephts, Armatoles and Pirates in Macedonia during the Rule of the Turks (1627–1821)* (Thessaloniki, 1975), pp. 98–100.

11. *Messager d'Athenes,* June 9, 1925.

12. K. Karpat, *Ottoman Population, 1830–1914* (Madison, Wisc., 1985), pp. 4–5, 22–23; J. Lampe and M. Jackson, *Balkan Economic History, 1550–1950* (Bloomington, Ind., 1982), p. 281; Ramberti, in L. Villari, *The Republic of Ragusa: An Episode of the Turkish Conquest* (London, 1904); W. Lithgow, *Rare Adventures and Painefull Peregrinations* (1632; reprint, London, 1928), p. 105.

13. On returning Christians, see H. Lowry, "The Island of Limnos: A Case Study on the Continuity of Byzantine Forms under Ottoman Rule," in H. Lowry, *Studies in Defterology* (Istanbul, 1992), pp. 181–209.

14. *The Negotiations of Sir Thomas Roe in His Embassy to the Ottoman Porte from the Year 1621 to 1628 Inclusive…* (London, 1740), p. 427; K. Kostis, *Ston kairo tis panolis* (Heraklion, Greece, 1995); D. Panzac, *La Peste dans l'Empire ottoman, 1700–1850* (Louvain, Belgium, 1985), esp. pp. 64–66.

15. The best account is M. Todorova, "Les Balkans" in J.-P. Bardet and J. Dupaquier, eds., *Histoire des populations de l'Europe* (Paris, 1998), vol. 2, pp. 465–87; long-run population figures in C. McEvedy and R. Jones, *Atlas of World Population History* (London, 1978), pp. 19, 95–99, 110–115. On Balkan populations, see also for the nineteenth century M. Palairet, *The Balkan Economies, c. 1800–1914: Evolution without Development* (Cambridge, 1997), pp. 6–14; H. Inalcik and D. Quataert, eds., *An Economic and Social History of the Ottoman Empire, 1300–1914* (Cambridge, 1994), p. 652; Royal Institute of International Affairs, *Southeastern Europe* (London, 1940), p. 85.

16. Warriner, *Contrasts*, p. 142; K. Hitchins, *The Romanians, 1774–1866* (Oxford, 1996), p. 173.

17. A. Wace and M. Thompson, *The Nomads of the Balkans* (London, 1914), p. 33.

18. A. Goff and H. A. Fawcett, *Macedonia: A Plea for the Primitive* (London, 1921), pp. xiv–xv, 8.

19. Stoianovich, *Balkan Worlds*, pp. 248–49; on Wallachian hovels, see Tietz, *St. Petersburgh*, p. 78; on Bulgarian huts, see H. Pernot, ed., *Voyage en Turquie et en Grece de Robert de Dreux* (Paris, 1925), p. 95. My thanks to Heath Lowry for information about Ottoman clocks.

20. T. Stoianovich, "Land Tenure and Related Sectors of the Balkan Economy," in T. Stoianovich, *Between East and West: The Balkan and Mediterranean Worlds* (New Rochelle, N.Y., 1992), vol. 1, pp. 1–15.

21. P. Sugar, "The Least Affected Social Group in the Ottoman Balkans: The Peasantry," in S. Vryonis, ed., *Byzantine Studies: Essays on the Slavic World and the Eleventh Century* (New York, 1992), pp. 77–87.

22. B. McGowan, *Economic Life in Ottoman Europe: Taxation, Trade and the Struggle for Land, 1600–1800* (Cambridge, 1981), pp. 54–55.

23. For Ottoman continuation of Byzantine land taxes, see S. Vryonis, "Byzantium and Islam: Seventh–Seventeenth Century," in *Byzantine Studies* IX: pp. 234–35; Inalcik and Quataert, *Economic and Social History*, p. 159.

24. Cited by S. Fischer-Galati, ed., *Man, State and Society in East European History* (New York, 1970), p. 73.

25. See G. Veinstein, "On the Ciftlik Debate," in C. Keydar and F. Tabak, eds., *Landholding and Commercial Agriculture in the Middle East* (Albany, N.Y., 1991), pp. 35–57; T. Stoianovich, "Balkan Peasants, Landlords

and the Ottoman State," in op. cit., pp. 15–39; Inalcik and Quataert, *Economic and Social History,* p. 45; for a Greek Christian case, see G. Veinstein, "Le Patrimoine foncier de Panayote Benakis, Kocabasi de Kalamata," in G. Veinstein, *Etat et société dans l'Empire ottoman, XVIe–XVIIIe siècles* (Aldershot, Eng., 1994), vol. 3, pp. 211–33.

26. J. R. McNeill, *The Mountains of the Mediterranean World: An Environmental History* (Cambridge, 1992), pp. 89–90; M. E. Durham, *Some Tribal Origins, Laws and Customs of the Balkans* (London, 1928), p. 273.

27. Kantemir quoted in Warriner, *Contrasts,* p. 128; B. Brue, *Journal de la campagne que le Grand Vezir Ali Pacha a faite en 1715 pour la conquete de la Morée* (Paris, 1870), p. 38.

28. J. Koliopoulos, *Brigands with a Cause: Brigandage and Irredentism in Modern Greece, 1821–1912* (Oxford, 1987), p. 239; D. Urquhart, *The Spirit of the East, Illustrated in a Journal of Travels through Roumeli during an Eventful Period* (London, 1838), vol. 2, p. 150.

29. Urquhart, *Spirit of the East,* vol. 2, pp. 157, 162–63.

30. McGowan, *Economic Life,* p. 65; F. Adanir, "Tradition and Rural Change in Southeastern Europe during Ottoman Rule," in D. Chirot, ed., *The Origins of Backwardness in Eastern Europe* (Berkeley, 1989), p. 135.

31. Leake cited in Inalcik and Quataert, *Economic and Social History,* p. 689.

32. H. Lowry, "From Lesser Wars to the Mightiest War: The Ottoman Conquest and Transformation of Byzantine Urban Centers in the Fifteenth Century," in Lowry, *Studies in Defterology,* pp. 47–65.

33. S. Vryonis, "Religious Change and Continuity in the Balkans and Anatolia from the Fourteenth through the Seventeenth Century," in S. Vryonis, ed., *Islam and Cultural Change in the Middle Ages* (Wiesbaden, 1975), pp. 130–32.

34. Cf. M. Kiel, *Studies on the Ottoman Architecture of the Balkans* (Aldershot, Eng., 1990), introduction; and S. Curcic and E. Hadjitryphonos, eds., *Secular Medieval Architecture in the Balkans, 1300–1500, and Its Preservation* (Thessaloniki, 1997). For population figures, see "Istanbul," *Encyclopaedia of Islam,* vol. 4, p. 226–46, and, for other cities, J. de Vries, *European Urbanization, 1500–1800* (Cambridge, Mass., 1984), pp. 270–87; Lithgow, *Rare Adventures,* p. 179; Halsband, *Complete Letters,* vol. 1, p. 354.

35. T. Stoianovich, "Model and Mirror of the Premodern Balkan City"

in T. Stoianovich, *Between East and West: The Balkan and Mediterranean Worlds,* vol. 2, *Economies and Societies* (New Rochelle, N.Y., 1992), p. 108; see also his "The Conquering Balkan Orthodox Merchant" in ibid., pp. 1–77.

36. Stoianovich, *Balkan Worlds,* p. 75; *Negotiations of Sir Thomas Roe,* p. 67; Tietz, *St. Petersburgh,* p. 79; J. J. Best, *Excursions in Albania* (London, 1842), p. 188; Warriner, *Contrasts,* p. 146; H. Andonov-Poljansky, ed., *British Documents on the History of the Macedonian People* (Skopje, 1968), vol. 1, p. 287.

37. Stoianovich, "Balkan Peasants, Landlords," p. 30.

38. Ibid., p. 38, n. 80; Evans, *Through Bosnia,* pp. 334–36.

39. Blanqui in Warriner, *Contrasts,* pp. 216, 244; W. Smyth, *A Year with the Turks* (New York, 1854), p. 224.

40. J. K. Campbell, *Honour, Family and Patronage* (Oxford, 1964), p. 15.

41. R. Bicanic, *How the People Live: Life in the Passive Regions* (Amherst, Mass., 1981), p. 52; Lampe and Jackson, *Balkan Economic History,* pp. 193–94; H. L. Roberts, *Rumania: Political Problems of an Agrarian State* (New York, 1969), pp. 3–9.

42. C. Bracewell, *The Uskoks of Senj: Piracy, Banditry and Holy War in the Sixteenth Century Adriatic* (Ithaca, N.Y., 1992), p. 31; Djilas, *Land without Justice,* pp. 142, 201.

43. Warriner, *Contrasts,* p. 298; Palairet, *Balkan Economies,* p. 122; on the village, see N. Iorga, *Etudes Byzantines* (Bucharest, 1939), vol. 1, p. 172.

44. A. Hulme Beaman, *Twenty Years in the Near East* (London, 1898), p. 121.

45. Bicanic, *How the People Live,* pp. 121–23; K. Mandelbaum, *The Industrialisation of Backward Areas* (Oxford, 1945), p. 2.

46. S. Runciman, "Balkan Cities—Yesterday and Today," in D. W. Hoover and J. Koumoulides, eds., *Cities in History* (Muncie, Ind., 1977), pp. 1–13.

2. BEFORE THE NATION

1. M. Avgerinos, *Makedonika apomnimonevmata* (Athens, 1914), p. 10.

2. E. Durham, *The Burden of the Balkans* (London, 1905), pp. 143–44.

3. H. N. Brailsford, *Macedonia: Its Races and Their Future* (London, 1906), pp. 99–100.

4. H. Lowther to E. Grey, October 2, 1912, in B. Destani, ed., *Albania*

and Kosovo: Political and Ethnic Boundaries, 1867–1946 (London, 1999), p. 292.

5. P. Charanis, "Ethnic Changes in Seventh-Century Byzantium" in P. Charanis, *Studies on the Demography of the Byzantine Empire: Collected Studies* (London, 1972), pp. 36–38.

6. D. Zakythinos, "Byzance et les peuples de l'Europe du sud-est: La synthèse byzantine," in D. Zakythinos, *Byzance: Etat-société-economie* (London, 1973), vol. 6, p. 13; on Greek in Romania, see S. Story, ed., *Memoirs of Ismail Kemal Bey* (London, 1920), p. 21; A. Smith, *Glimpses of Greek Life and Scenery* (London, 1884); A. Ducellier, *Oi alvanoi stin Ellada (13os–15os aion.)* (Athens, 1994).

7. See T. Stavrides, "The Ottoman Grand Vezir Mahmud Pasha Angelovic (1453–1474)" (Ph.D. diss., Harvard University, 1996).

8. C. H. Fleischer, *Bureaucrat and Intellectual in the Ottoman Empire: The Historian Mustafa Ali (1541–1600)* (Princeton, N.J., 1986), pp. 158–59; Symeon in M. Balivet, "Aux origins de l'islamisation des Balkans Ottomans," *Revue du Monde Musulman et de la Méditerranée* 66, no. 4 (1992), p. 13; Sandys in S. Purchas, ed., *Purchas His Pilgrimes* (Glasgow, 1905), vol. 8, p. 123; H. C. Barkley, *Bulgaria before the War* (London, 1877), p. 179; W. Lithgow, *Rare Adventures and Painefull Peregrinations* (1632; reprint, London, 1928), p. 101; R. Halsband, ed., *The Complete Letters of Lady Mary Wortley Montagu, 1708–1720* (Oxford, 1965), p. 390.

9. R. Gradeva, "Ottoman Policy towards Christian Church Buildings," *Etudes Balkaniques* (1994), pp. 14–36; A. Handzic, *Population of Bosnia in the Ottoman Period* (Istanbul, 1994), p. 21.

10. H. F. Tozer, *Researches in the Highlands of Turkey* (London, 1869), vol. 1, p. 202; on Crete, see M. Greene, *A Shared World* (Princeton, N.J., 2000).

11. S. Vryonis, "Religious Change and Continuity in the Balkans and Anatolia from the Fourteenth through the Sixteenth Century," in S. Vryonis, ed., *Islam and Cultural Change in the Middle Ages* (Wiesbaden, 1975), pp. 127–41; P. Sugar, "The Least Affected Social Group in the Ottoman Balkans: The Peasantry," in S. Vryonis, ed., *Byzantine Studies: Essays on the Slavic World and the Eleventh Century* (New York, 1992), pp. 77–87; N. Sousa, *The Capitulatory Regime of Turkey: Its History, Origin, and Nature* (Baltimore, 1933), pp. 36ff.;

R. Jennings, *Christians and Muslims in Ottoman Cyprus and the Mediterranean World, 1571–1640* (New York, 1993), p. 143.

12. N. Filipovic, "A Contribution to the Problem of Islamicisation in the Balkans under Ottoman Rule," in *Ottoman Rule in Middle Europe and Balkan in the Sixteenth and Seventeenth Centuries* (Prague, 1978), pp. 305–59; N. Todorov, "The Demographic Situation in the Balkan Peninsula (Late Fifteenth–Early Sixteenth Century)," in N. Todorov, *Society, the City and Industry in the Balkans, Fifteenth–Nineteenth Centuries* (Aldershot, U.K., 1998), vol. 6.

13. On Catholic–Orthodox interaction, see L. Hadrovics, *Le Peuple serbe et son eglise sous la domination turque* (Paris, 1947), esp. p. 25; K. T. Ware, "Orthodox and Catholics in the Seventeenth Century: Schism or Intercommunion?" in D. Baker, ed., *Schism, Heresy and Religious Protest* (Cambridge, 1972), pp. 259–76; G. Hoffmann, *Vescovadi Cattolici della Grecia* (Rome, 1937–1941), vols. 2–5.

14. T. H. Papadopoulos, *Studies and Documents Relating to the History of the Greek Church and People Under Turkish Domination* (Brussels, 1952), pp. 10–26; Hadrovics, *Le Peuple serb,* pp. 95–96. For an important reassessment of the millet system, see P. Konortas, "From Ta'ife to Millet: Ottoman Terms for the Ottoman Greek Orthodox Community," in D. Gondicas and C. Issawi, eds., *Orthodox Greeks in the Age of Nationalism* (Princeton, N.J., 1999), pp. 169–81, and also B. Braude and B. Lewis, eds., *Christians and Jews in the Ottoman Empire: The Functioning of a Plural Society* (New York, 1982).

15. Crusius cited by S. Runciman, *The Great Church in Captivity* (Cambridge, 1968), p. 180; L. Stavrianos, *The Balkans since 1453* (New York, 1965), p. 181.

16. P. Mansel, *Constantinople: City of the World's Desire, 1453–1924* (London, 1995), p. 148; R. Abou-el-Haj, "Ottoman Diplomacy at Karlowitz," *Journal of the American Oriental Society* 87, no. 4 (1967), pp. 498–512; C. Mango, "The Phanariots and the Byzantine Tradition," in R. Clogg, ed., *The Struggle for Greek Independence* (London, 1973), p. 51.

17. Runciman, *Great Church,* p. 391; Stavrianos, *Balkans since 1453,* p. 225; A. J. Evans, *Through Bosnia and the Herzegovina on Foot* (London, 1877), pp. 267–68.

18. P. Kitromilides, "Cultural Change and Social Criticism: The Case of

Iosipos Moisiodax," in P. Kitromilides, *Enlightenment, Nationalism, Orthodoxy: Studies in the Culture and Political Thought of Southeastern Europe* (Aldershot, Eng., 1994), p. 671, and his " 'Balkan Mentality': History, Legend, Imagination," *Nations and Nationalism* 2, no. 22 (1996), pp. 163–91; C. Dawson, *The Making of Europe* (London, 1946), p. 147; S. Batalden, *Catherine II's Greek Prelate: Eugenios Voulgaris in Russia, 1771–1806* (Boulder, Colo., 1982); Mango, "Phanariots and Byzantine Tradition," pp. 41–67.

19. Lithgow, *Rare Adventures*, p. 76.

20. *New Martyrs of the Turkish Yoke* (Seattle, 1985), p. 321; Fleischer, *Bureaucrat and Intellectual*, pp. 62–63.

21. E. S. Forster, ed., *The Turkish Letters of Ghiselin de Busbecq* (Oxford, 1927), p. 136; H. Pernot, ed., *Voyage en Turquie et en Grece de Robert de Dreux* (Paris, 1925), p. 62; W. B. Stanford and E. J. Finopoulos, eds., *The Travels of Lord Charlemont in Greece and Turkey, 1749* (London, 1984), p. 39.

22. On Nikolaos of Metsovo, see *New Martyrs*, pp. 185–87; on Cyprus, see Jennings, *Christians and Muslims*, pp. 179–81; Tozer, *Researches*, vol. 2, p. 80; S. Lane Poole, *The People of Turkey* (London, 1878), vol. 2, p. 225.

23. M. E. Durham, *Some Tribal Origins, Laws and Customs of the Balkans* (London, 1928), pp. 244–61.

24. Boscovich cited in L. Wolff, *Inventing Eastern Europe* (Stanford, Calif., 1994), p. 175; W. Smyth, *A Year with the Turks* (New York, 1854), p. 22.

25. D. Loukopoulos, *Georgika tis Roumelis* (Athens, 1938), pp. 163–64; C. Bracewell, *The Uskoks of Senj: Piracy, Banditry and Holy War in the Sixteenth Century Adriatic* (Ithaca, N.Y., 1992), pp. 158–59, n. 12; Tozer, *Researches*, vol. 1, pp. 206–7; L. Edwards, ed., *The Memoirs of Prota Matija Nenadovic* (Oxford, 1969), p. 17.

26. G. Rouillard, *La Vie rurale dans l'Empire byzantine* (Paris, 1953), p. 199; cf., for useful methodological remarks, V. Shevzov, "Chapels and the Ecclesial World of Prerevolutionary Peasants," *Slavic Review* 55, no. 3 (Fall 1996), pp. 584–613, and C. Chulos, "Myths of the Pious or Pagan Peasant in Post-Emancipation Central Russia (Voronezh Province)," *Russian History* 22, no. 2 (Summer 1995), pp. 181–216. My thanks to Laura Engelstein for these references.

27. Cited in Balivet, "Aux origins," p. 18; see the work of W. Christian,

especially *Local Religion in Sixteenth-Century Spain* (Princeton, N.J., 1981). My thanks to Ken Mills for this reference. Forster, *Busbecq*, pp. 136–37.

28. A "shared world" comes from M. Greene's new *A Shared World* (Princeton, N.J., 2000), N. Todorov, "Traditions et transformations dans les villes balkaniques avec l'instauration de l'Empire ottoman" in Todorov, *Society, the City*, vol. 3, p. 99; Jennings, *Christians and Muslims*, pp. 134, 142.

29. B. F. Musallam, *Sex and Society in Islam* (Cambridge, 1983); Purchas, *Purchas His Pilgrimes*, vol. 8 p. 276; N. Pantazopoulos, *Church and Law in the Balkan Peninsula during Ottoman Rule*, in *Epistimoniki epeterida: Anticharisma ston Nikolao I. Pantazopoulo* (Thessaloniki, 1986), vol. 3, pp. 327–29; Stanford and Finopoulos, *Lord Charlemont*, pp. 48–49. The practice of kepinion is also described in the seventeenth-century accounts of Thevenot and Sir Paul Rycaut, *The Present State of the Greek and Armenian Churches anno Christi, 1678* (New York, 1970).

30. F. Babinger, *Mehmed the Conqueror and His Time* (Princeton, N.J., 1978), pp. 16–18; Story, *Memoirs of Ismail Kemal Pasha*, p. 38.

31. Jennings, *Christians and Muslims*, p. 29; Greene, *A Shared World*; C. Imber, "'Involuntary' Annulment of Marriage and Its Solutions in Ottoman Law" in C. Imber, *Studies in Ottoman History and Law* (Istanbul, 1996), p. 226.

32. R. Dankoff, trans., *The Intimate Life of an Ottoman Statesman Melek Ahmed Pasha (1588–1662), as Portrayed in Evliya Celebi's Book of Travels (Seyahat-Name)* (Albany, N.Y., 1991), pp. 249–50; see also Bracewell, *Uskoks*, pp. 181–82.

33. F. W. Hasluck, *Christianity and Islam under the Sultans* (Oxford, 1929), vol. 2, p. 554; Durham, *Burden of the Balkans*, p. 356.

34. Durham, *Burden of the Balkans*, p. 51.

35. *New Martyrs*, p. 39; Durham, *Some Tribal Origins*, pp. 290–91.

36. Ramsay cited in V. N. Dadrian, *The History of the Armenian Genocide* (Providence, R.I., 1995), p. 158; M. von Tietz, *St. Petersburgh, Constantinople and Napoli di Romania in 1833 and 1834* (New York, 1836), p. 135, citing an unnamed earlier traveler; Jennings, *Christians and Muslims*, p. 101.

37. Gradeva, "Ottoman Policy Towards Christian Church Buildings," pp. 14–35; J. V. de la Roiere, *Voyage en Orient* (Paris, 1836), p. 273.

38. D. Warriner, ed., *Contrasts in Emerging Societies: Readings in the Social and Economic History of South-Eastern Europe in the Nineteenth Century* (London, 1965), p. 234.

39. S. Deringil, *The Well-Protected Domains: Ideology and the Legitimation of Power in the Ottoman Empire, 1876–1909* (London, 1999), p. 115.

40. "Martyrdom of Holy New Hieromartyr, Serafim, Bishop of Phanarion," in *New Martyrs*, p. 361.

41. F. Venturi, *The End of the Old Regime in Europe, 1768–1776* (Princeton, N.J., 1989), pp. 10–29.

42. G. Finlay, *The History of Greece under Ottoman and Venetian Domination* (London, 1861), pp. 323–24; Varlaam cited by T. Prousis, *Russian Society and the Greek Revolution* (De Kalb, Ill., 1994), p. 6; T. Blancard, *Les Mavroyeni* (Paris, 1909), vol. 3, pp. 84–85; Dapontes in Mango, "Phanariots and Byzantine Tradition," p. 55.

43. C. Koumarianou, "The Contribution of the Intelligentsia towards the Greek Independence Movement, 1798–1821," in Clogg, *Struggle for Greek Independence*, p. 70.

44. P. Kitromilides, "The Enlightenment East and West: A Comparative Perspective on the Ideological Origins of the Balkan Political Traditions," in Kitromilides, *Enlightenment, Nationalism, Orthodoxy*, pp. 51–70; R. Clogg, "Aspects of the Movement for Greek Independence," in Clogg, *Struggle for Greek Independence*, p. 26.

45. Text in R. Clogg, ed., *The Movement for Greek Independence, 1770–1821* (London, 1976), pp. 157–63.

46. Clogg, "Aspects," pp. 25–29; Clogg, *Movement*, pp. 58–61, 89–90.

47. P. Khilandarski cited by Clogg, "Aspects," p. 21; on the Romanian Enlightenment, see K. Hitchins, *The Rumanian National Movement in Transylvania, 1780–1849* (Cambridge, Mass., 1969).

48. P. Sugar and I. Lederer, eds., *Nationalism in Eastern Europe* (Seattle, 1969), pp. 105–6, 373–79, 401–2.

49. P. Kitromilides, " 'Imagined Communities' and the Origins of the National Question in the Balkans," in Kitromilides, *Enlightenment, Nationalism, Orthodoxy*, pp. xi, 158.

50. C. Frazee, *The Orthodox Church and Independent Greece, 1821–1852* (Cambridge, 1969), p. 31.

51. Ibid., p. 188; P. Ramet, ed., *Eastern Christianity and Politics in the Twentieth Century* (Durham, N.C., 1988), pp. 10–11.

52. On missionaries, J. Clarke, *American Missionaries and the National Revival of Bulgaria* (1939; reprint, New York, 1971), pp. 233–34; Runciman, *Great Church*, p. 396.

3. EASTERN QUESTIONS

1. P. B. Shelley, *Hellas*, 1822.
2. L. von Ranke, *The History of Servia and the Servian Revolution* (London, 1853), p. 365.
3. T. G. Djuvara, *Cents projets de partage de la Turquie* (Paris, 1914).
4. Ibid., pp. 278–305.
5. Kolokotrónis cited by L. Stavrianos, *The Balkans since 1453* (New York, 1965), p. 212; H. Temperley, *England and the Near East: The Crimea* (London, 1936), p. 57.
6. A. Suceska, "The Eighteenth Century Austro-Ottoman Wars' Economic Impact on the Population of Bosnia," in G. Rothernberg et al., eds., *East Central European Society and War in the Pre-Revolutionary Eighteenth Century* (New York, 1982), pp. 339–48; H. Andonov-Poljanski, ed., *British Documents on the History of the Macedonian People* (Skopje, 1968), vol. 1, p. 180.
7. Ranke, *History of Servia*, p. 66.
8. L. Edwards, ed., *The Memoirs of Prota Matija Nenadovic* (Oxford, 1969), p. 192.
9. Ranke, *History of Servia*, pp. 188–99; W. Vucinich, ed., *The First Serbian Uprising, 1804–1813* (New York, 1982).
10. D. Skiotis, "The Greek Revolution: Ali Pacha's Last Gamble," in N. Diamandouros, ed., *Hellenism and the First Greek War of Liberation* (Thessaloniki, 1976), pp. 97–109; K. Fleming, *The Muslim Bonaparte: Diplomacy and Orientalism in Ali Pasha's Greece* (Princeton, N.J., 1999).
11. Cited in T. Prousis, *Russian Society and the Greek Revolution* (De Kalb, Ill., 1994), pp. 139–40.
12. B. Jelavich, *Russia's Balkan Entanglements, 1806–1914* (Cambridge, 1993), pp. 49–75.
13. H. A. Lidderdale, trans., *Makriyannis: The Memoirs of General Makriyannis, 1797–1864* (Oxford, 1966), p. 14; Andonov-Poljanski, *British Documents*, vol. 1, p. 221; T. Kolokotrónis, *Memoirs from the Greek War of Independence, 1821–1833* (London, 1892), p. 157.

14. Prousis, *Russian Society,* p. 51; J. R. Marriott, *The Eastern Question: An Historical Study in European Diplomacy* (Oxford, 1917), p. 214.

15. Andonov-Poljanski, *British Documents,* vol. 1, p. 264.

16. Vucinich, *First Serb Uprising,* p. 251.

17. J. A. Blanqui, *Voyage en Bulgarie pendant l'année 1844* (Paris, 1845), p. 67; on urban planning in the Ottoman Balkans, see A. Karadimou-Gerolympou, *I anoikodomisi tis Thessalonikis meta tin pyrkaia tou 1917* (Thessaloniki, 1995).

18. Blanqui, *Voyage en Bulgarie,* p. 93.

19. Jelavich, *Russia's Balkan Entanglements,* pp. 75–90; B. Jelavich, *History of the Balkans* (Cambridge, 1983), vol. 1, p. 265.

20. K. Hitchins, *The Romanians, 1781–1866* (Oxford, 1996), pp. 161–66; C. Giurescu, *History of Bucharest* (Bucharest, 1976), pp. 48–51.

21. F. Kellogg, *The Road to Romanian Independence* (West Lafayette, Ind., 1995), p. 5.

22. M. Pinson, "Ottoman Bulgaria in the First Tanzimat Period: The Revolts in Nish (1841) and Vidin (1850)," *Middle Eastern Studies* 11, no. 2 (May 1975), pp. 103–46; Odysseus [Sir Charles Eliot], *Turkey in Europe* (London, 1900), p. 347; M. Macdermott, *A History of Bulgaria, 1393–1885* (New York, 1962), p. 124.

23. Jelavich, *History of Balkans,* vol. 1, pp. 340–41.

24. J. F. Clarke, *Bible Societies, American Missionaries and the National Revival of Bulgaria* (1937; reprint, New York, 1971); Macdermott, *History of Bulgaria,* pp. 194–95.

25. Jelavich, *History of Balkans,* vol. 1, p. 347.

26. On the political pressure exerted by irredentists, see J. Koliopoulos, *Brigands with a Cause: Brigandage and Irredentism in Modern Greece, 1821–1912* (Oxford, 1987).

27. Eliot, *Turkey in Europe,* p. 271.

28. D. Livanios, " 'Conquering the Souls': Nationalism and Greek Guerilla Warfare in Ottoman Macedonia, 1904–1908," *Byzantine and Modern Greek Studies* 23 (1999), pp. 195–221.

29. A. Rappoport, *Au pays des martyrs: Notes et souvenirs d'un ancien consul general d'Autriche-Hongrie en Macedoine (1904–1909)* (Paris, 1927), p. 18.

30. *British Documents on Foreign Affairs,* part 1, series B, vol. 19 (Bethesda, Md., 1985), pp. 500–507.

31. H. C. Barkley, *Bulgaria before the War* (London, 1877), p. 272.

32. J. Baernreither, *Fragments of a Political Diary* (London, 1930), pp. 22–27, 51, 126.

33. B. Schmitt, *The Annexation of Bosnia, 1908–1909* (Cambridge, 1937).

34. V. Dedijer, *The Road to Sarajevo* (London, 1966); Baernreither, *Fragments,* pp. 244–46.

35. H. Lowther to E. Grey, October 2, 1912, in B. Destani, ed., *Albania and Kosovo: Political and Ethnic Boundaries, 1867–1946* (London, 1999), p. 292.

36. L. Stavrianos, *The Balkans since 1453* (rev. ed., London, 2000), p. 535.

37. R. W. Seton-Watson, *A History of the Roumanians* (Cambridge, 1934), ch. 16; N. Stone, *The Eastern Front* (London, 1975), pp. 71, 264, 277.

38. D. Lloyd George, *War Memoirs,* vol. 2 (London, n.d.).

39. Mansel, *Constantinople: City of the World's Desire, 1453–1924* (London, 1995), p. 408.

40. K. Calder, *Britain and the Origins of the New Europe, 1914–1918* (Cambridge, 1976), p. 16.

41. I. Banac, *The National Question in Yugoslavia* (Ithaca, N.Y., 1984).

4. Building the Nation-State

1. Cited in J. D. Bell, *Peasants in Power: Alexander Stamboliski and the Bulgarian Agrarian National Union, 1899–1923* (Princeton, N.J., 1977), p. 4.

2. V. Dedijer, *The Road to Sarajevo* (London, 1966), p. 73; O. Jaszi, "The Irresistibility of the National Idea," in O. Jaszi, *Homage to Danubia* (Lanham, Md., 1994).

3. M. S. Anderson, *The Great Powers and the Near East, 1774–1923* (London, 1970), p. 32; Naval Intelligence Division, *Jugoslavia* (n.p., 1944), vol. 2, pp. 104–7.

4. A. Toumarkine, *Les Migrations des populations musulmanes balkaniques en Anatolie (1876–1913)* (Istanbul, 1995), pp. 27–50.

5. On the Romanian constitution, see K. Hitchins, *Rumania, 1866–1947* (Oxford, 1994), pp. 16–17; P. Michelson, *Conflict and Crisis: Romanian Political Development, 1861–1871* (New York, 1987).

6. *Report of the International Commission to Inquire into the Causes and Conduct of the Balkan Wars* (Washington, D.C., 1914), pp. 154–55.

7. F. Fellner, ed., *Das politische tagebuch Josef Redlichs* (Vienna, 1953), vol. 1, pp. 280, 289; HMSO, *The Jugoslav Movement* (London, 1920), pp. 21–23.

8. M. Mazower, "Minorities and the League of Nations in Interwar Europe," *Daedalus,* 126, no. 2 (Spring 1997), pp. 47–65.

9. For Greek documents on this dispute, see B. Kondis and E. Manda, eds., *The Greek Minority in Albania: A Documentary Record (1921–1993)* (Thessaloniki, 1994).

10. H. Pozzi, *Black Hand over Europe* (London, 1935), p. 181.

11. O. Janowsky, *People at Bay: The Jewish Problem in East-Central Europe* (Oxford, 1938).

12. R. Lemkin, *Axis Rule in Occupied Europe* (Washington, D.C., 1944), pp. 612, 626–27; A. Djilas, *The Contested Country: Yugoslav Unity and Communist Revolution, 1919–1953* (Cambridge, Mass., 1991), ch. 4.

13. On Chetniks, see I. Banac, "Bosnian Muslims: From Religious Community to Socialist Nationhood and Post-Communist Statehood, 1918–1992," in M. Pinson, ed., *The Muslims of Bosnia-Herzegovina* (Cambridge, Mass., 1994), pp. 142–43.

14. N. Malcolm, *Kosovo: A Short History* (London, 1998), p. 312; J. Koliopoulos, *Plundered Loyalties: World War II and Civil War in Greek West Macedonia* (New York, 1999).

15. R. King, *Minorities under Communism: Nationalities as a Source of Tension among Balkan Communist States* (Cambridge, Mass., 1973); P. Shoup, *Communism and the Yugoslav National Question* (New York, 1968).

16. D. Mitrany, *Marx against the Peasant* (Chapel Hill, N.C., 1951), p. 118.

17. H. Tiltman, *Peasant Europe* (London, 1937).

18. For a case study, see M. Mazower, *Greece and the Interwar Economic Crisis* (Oxford, 1991).

19. Hoare to Halifax, July 5, 1940, British Documents on Foreign Affairs, vol. 21, 23:5 (Bethesda, Md., 1998), ch. 5, n. 55. I am indebted to Kate Thirolf for this reference.

20. E. Barker, *Truce in the Balkans* (London, 1948), p. 255.

21. Ibid.; H. Seton-Watson, *The East European Revolution* (London, 1954), pp. 254–55, 335, 388.

22. R. L. Wolff, *The Balkans in Our Time* (New York, 1978), ch. 14; M. E. Fischer, "Politics, Nationalism and Development in Romania," in G. Augustinos, ed., *Diverse Paths to Modernity in Southeastern Europe* (New York, 1991), p. 149.

23. E. Stillman, *The Balkans* (New York, 1966), p. 146; W. H. McNeill, *The Metamorphosis of Greece since World War II* (Oxford, 1978), p. 247.

24. N. V. Giannaris, *Geopolitical and Economic Changes in the Balkan Countries* (London, 1996); Fischer, "Politics, Nationalism and Development," p. 157; C. Deltuere de Brycher, "Quelques images de la systematisation," in N. Pelisser et al., eds., *La Roumanie contemporaine* (Paris, 1996), pp. 13–49.

25. F. Fejto, *A History of the People's Democracies* (Harmondsworth, Eng., 1974), pp. 376–77.

26. J. Lampe, "Belated Modernization in Comparison: Development in Yugoslavia and Bulgaria to 1948," in Augustinos, *Diverse Paths to Modernity*, pp. 32–45.

27. Cited in King, *Minorities under Communism*, p. 21.

28. G. Stokes, *From Stalinism to Pluralism: A Documentary History of Eastern Europe since 1945* (New York, 1991), pp. 232–33; H. Poulton, *The Balkans: Minorities and States in Conflict* (London, 1991), pp. 112–13, 126, 131, 153–65.

EPILOGUE

1. An Ottoman official cited in J. Mislin, *Les Saints Lieux: Pelerinage à Jerusalem* (Paris, 1876), vol. 1, p. 72.

2. Both quotes are from M. Levene, "Introduction," in M. Levene and P. Roberts, eds., *The Massacre in History* (New York, 1999).

3. A. J. Toynbee, *The Western Question in Greece and Turkey* (London, 1922), pp. 17–18.

4. "Verdict against SS-Untersturmführer Max Taeubner, 24 May 1943," in E. Klee, W. Dressen and V. Riess, eds., *"Those Were the Days": The Holocaust as Seen by the Perpetrators and By-standers* (London, 1991), pp. 196–207; on rules of war, see G. Best, *Humanity in Warfare* (Oxford, 1980); on the civilizing process, the classic work is N. Elias, *The Civilising Process* (Oxford, 1978).

5. Montaigne, translated by John Florio, "Of Crueltie" in *The Essays of Michael Lord of Montaigne* (Oxford, 1906), vol. 2, p. 134.

6. Gatrell, *Hanging Tree: Execution and the English People, 1770–1868* (Oxford, 1994), p. 598; also T. Haskell, "Capitalism and the Origins of the Humanitarian Sensibility," *American Historical Review* 90, no. 2–3 (April/June 1985), pp. 339–61 and 547–66. My thanks to Liz Lunbeck for this reference.

7. J. Gardner Wilkinson, *Dalmatia and Montenegro* (London, 1848), pp. 80–82.

8. P. P. Njegos, *The Mountain Wreath*, trans. V. Mihailovich (Irvine, Calif., 1986), and also M. Sells, *The Bridge Betrayed: Religion and Genocide in Bosnia* (Los Angeles, 1996), pp. 40–42. The Vladika's brother and cousins had been decapitated by Turks in 1836 before being suitably avenged four years later: M. Aubin, *Visions historiques et politiques dans l'oeuvre poetique de P. P. Njegos* (Paris, 1972), pp. 175–78; on Turkish attitudes to dissections, see the memoirs of an American surgeon in Ottoman service, J. O. Noyes, *Romania: The Borderland of the Christian and the Turk* (New York, 1857), p. 263.

9. Z. Milch, *A Stranger's Supper: An Oral History of Centenarian Women in Montenegro* (New York, 1995), p. 47; G. Stokes, *Politics as Development: The Emergence of Political Parties in Nineteenth-Century Serbia* (Durham, N.C., 1990), p. 147.

10. See also C. Boehm, *Blood Revenge: The Anthropology of Feuding in Montenegro and Other Tribal Societies* (Lawrence, Kans., 1984).

11. *Daily Mirror*, November 10, 1947; correspondence in Public Records Office, FO 371/67011, R 15110, Norton to London, November 12, 1947. I am greatly indebted to Polymeris Voglis for this information. J. Axtell and W. C. Sturtevant, "The Unkindest Cut, or Who Invented Scalping?" *William and Mary Quarterly* 37, no. 3 (July 1980), pp. 451–72.

12. Figures from United Nations (G. Newman, ed.), *Global Report on Crime and Justice* (New York, 1999); R. Hood, *The Death Penalty: A World-Wide Perspective* (Oxford, 1996), p. 74.

13. On Njegos, see Aubin, *Visions historiques*, pp. 232–35.

14. My thanks to Polymeris Voglis for this point. See also M. Ignatieff, *Virtual War* (London, 2000); on the Second World War as a civil war and forms of violence, see C. Pavone, *Una guerra civilie: Saggio sulla moralita nella resistenza* (Turin, 1991).

Guide to Further Reading

The outstanding textbook on the history of the Balkans is L. S. Stavrianos, *The Balkans since 1453* (1958; reprint, New York, 1965), a book that has now been reissued (London, 2000). Also valuable on the eighteenth and nineteenth centuries is G. Castellan, *History of the Balkans* (New York, 1992), and on the first half of the twentieth century, R. L. Wolff, *The Balkans in Our Time* (New York, 1956; rev. ed. 1978). B. Jelavich, *History of the Balkans*, 2 vols. (Cambridge, 1983), is solid on political and diplomatic developments. C. and B. Jelavich, eds., *The Balkans in Transition: Essays on the Development of Balkan Life and Politics since the Eighteenth Century* (Berkeley, 1963) is an important collection of essays. Their *The Establishment of the Balkan National States, 1804–1920* (Seattle, 1977) is also useful. T. Stoianovich, *Balkan Worlds: The First and Last Europe* (New York, 1994), offers many useful insights by an eminent social historian.

On geography, there is F. W. Carter, *An Historical Geography of the Balkans* (London, 1977); and J. Cvijic, *La Peninsule balkanique: Géographie humaine* (Paris, 1918). M. Todorova, *Imagining the Balkans* (New York, 1997) covers Western stereotypes of the region. On economic history: J. Lampe and M. Jackson, *Balkan Economic History, 1550–1950* (Bloomington, Ind., 1982); M. Palairet, *The Balkan Economies, c. 1800–1914: Evolution without Development* (Cambridge, 1997); T. Stoianovich, *Between East and West: The Balkan and Mediterranean Worlds,* 4 vols. (New Rochelle, N.Y., 1992–1995); and N. Todorov, *The Balkan City, 1400–1900* (Seattle, 1983).

For earlier periods, consult J. Fine, *The Late Medieval Balkans: A Critical Survey from the Late Twelfth Century to the Ottoman Conquest* (Ann Arbor, Mich., 1987); P. Kitromilides, *Enlightenment, Nationalism, Orthodoxy: Studies in the Culture and Political Thought of Southeastern Europe* (Aldershot, Eng., 1994) and his *The Enlightenment as Social Criticism: Iosipos Moisiodax and Greek Culture in the Eighteenth Century* (Princeton, N.J., 1992); R. Clogg, ed., *Balkan Society in the Age of Greek Independence* (London, 1981); and D. Warriner, ed., *Contrasts in Emerging Societies: Readings in the Social and Economic History of South-Eastern Europe in the Nineteenth Century* (London, 1965).

On the Ottoman Balkans, there are P. Sugar, *Southeastern Europe under Ottoman Rule, 1354–1804* (Seattle, 1977); Odysseus (C. Eliot), *Turkey in Europe* (London, 1900); H. Inalcik, *The Ottoman Empire: The Classical Age, 1300–1600* (London, 1973); H. Inalcik and D. Quataert, eds.), *An Economic and Social History of the Ottoman Empire, 1300–1914* (Cambridge, 1994); F. Adanir, "Tradition and Rural Change in Southeastern Europe during Ottoman Rule," in D. Chirot, ed., *The Origins of Backwardness in Eastern Europe* (Berkeley, 1989); and W. Miller, *The Ottoman Empire and Its Successors, 1801–1927* (Cambridge, 1936) is still valuable. One must also mention the gripping account by C. Bracewell, *The Uskoks of Senj: Piracy, Banditry and Holy War in the Sixteenth Century Adriatic* (Ithaca, N.Y., 1992).

On Serbia: M. Petrovich, *A History of Modern Serbia, 1804–1918* (New York, 1976); on Yugoslavia, J. Lampe, *Yugoslavia as History: Twice There Was a Country* (Cambridge, 1996), and the outstanding monograph by Ivo Banac, *The National Question in Yugoslavia* (Ithaca, N.Y., 1984). Noel Malcolm has written two very useful books, *Bosnia: A Short History* (London, 1994) and *Kosovo: A Short History* (London, 1998). For Bulgaria, R. Crampton, *A Short History of Bulgaria* (Cambridge, 1987), his *Bulgaria, 1878–1918* (New York, 1983), and Mercia Macdermott, *A History of Bulgaria, 1393–1885* (New York,

1962); on Macedonia, H. N. Brailsford, *Macedonia: Its Races and Their Future* (London, 1906). For Greece, R. Clogg, *A Concise History of Greece* (Cambridge, 1992); J. Campbell and P. Sherrard, *Modern Greece* (London, 1968) is still very useful. On Romania, see H. Roberts, *Rumania: Political Problems of an Agrarian State* (New York, 1951); K. Hitchins, *Rumania, 1866–1947* (Oxford, 1994). On Albania, see S. Skendi, ed., *Albania* (New York, 1956) and his monograph, *The Albanian National Awakening, 1878–1912* (Princeton, N.J., 1967).

Among travel accounts and other pleasures, see S. Hyman, ed., *Edward Lear in the Levant: Travels in Albania, Greece and Turkey in Europe, 1848–1849* (London, 1988); the Turkish letters of Mary Wortley Montagu, and Ogier Ghiselin de Busbecq; as well as the writings of the great Victorian travelers, among whom may be mentioned Edith Durham, the Misses Mackenzie and Irby, Colonel W. M. Leake and the Reverend Henry Tozer. More recent memoirs include M. Djilas, *Land without Justice: An Autobiography of His Youth* (New York, 1958) and his *Wartime: With Tito and the Partisans* (New York, 1977) and R. G. Waldeck, *Athene Palace* (New York, 1942).

INDEX

A Note on the Type

The principal text of this Modern Library edition
was set in a digitized version of Janson,
a typeface that dates from about 1690 and was cut by Nicholas Kis,
a Hungarian working in Amsterdam. The original matrices have
survived and are held by the Stempel foundry in Germany.
Hermann Zapf redesigned some of the weights and sizes for Stempel,
basing his revisions on the original design.